Take
Time
To-Be

How learning to live in the moment allowed my brother to live an imperfect life, perfectly

by Nathan Hickman

Published by Hero Maker Publishing

Copyright © 2018 Nathan Hickman

All rights reserved.

ISBN-**13: 978-1-7328435-0-9**

Cover Design – Holly Clark

TABLE OF CONTENTS

THANK YOU

There are so many people to whom I am grateful. I recruited the dream-team of therapists and support and focused exclusively on my personal growth over the past years. I knew that the only thing keeping me from greatness was my own inner self.

Thank you, Dr. Khan of Pine Rest, for having the awareness I was overmedicated, and by eliminating certain medications, you would help my real self to come back online after being lost for more than a decade.

Thank you, Dr. Dan Post of Pine Rest, for helping me to see that my lack of connection was not a lack of connection to the world, but a lack of connection to myself. With this awareness, I found complete contentment.

Thank you, April Kaiserlian, April Kaiserlian *LCSW Therapy and Grand Rapids Center for Mindfulness*, for helping me understand that I'm privileged and still worthy of my struggles and for helping me to understand that life can be a both/and scenario. That life can be both hard and beautiful at the same time, that someone can be both privileged and at the same time struggle.

Thank you, Amina Knowlan, *The Matrix Leadership Institute*, for teaching me that by getting off the proverbial "Island of Me" and becoming connected with others, I would see that we are all struggling, and this would normalize my problems in a way that I no longer saw myself as bad or broken.

Thank you, Doug Kliewer, *The Hero Maker Group*, for giving me the confidence and courage to share my story. Without you, this book, and potentially my transformation, may not have taken place.

Thank you, Mom and Dad, for always making me feel special and important, a priority, for always being my rock and advocate, for never making me feel guilty for struggling, and for supporting and believing in me when I couldn't.

Chad, your life may have been shorter than expected, but your impact was profound and long-lasting. Thank you for teaching us how to live our best life. Your struggles and sacrifices have brought strength to an entire community. May your legacy live on forever.

"No matter how many times you get knocked down, you will always be a winner if you refuse to let life keep you down. It's not a matter if you will fall because at some point, you will. It's a matter of how many times you will fall and get back up. True greatness lies in those who will continually deny defeat."

— Nathan Hickman
(Quote inspired by Chad's life)

PROLOGUE

If you didn't know Chad Hickman, you would think he was shy and soft-spoken. Those of us lucky enough to know him intimately realized that inside that quiet youthful looking boy was a strong and determined young man.

Every moment of every day Chad was determined to succeed...although he was dealt an unenviable hand of cards, you never heard a complaint from him. Life continually knocked him down and he would gracefully get up, brush himself off, and find the will and strength to push on with extraordinary determination.

He had to learn to walk four times in his lifetime, and a month before he died at the age of 41, he had a rod put in his hip to prevent a complete break, and even though he was dying of cancer, he found the strength and pride in himself to do the impossible and learn to walk one last time. He took 19 steps.

As Dr. King said..."If you can't fly then run, if you can't run then walk, if you can't walk then crawl, but whatever you do, you have to keep moving forward." Chad never made excuses and always challenged himself to keep walking forward.

Chad taught the community how to live despite having the odds against him. Every day was a struggle, but those around him never knew it because he didn't complain, was grateful for what he did have, and for what he could do. He made the impossible possible simply by recognizing that he was in control of his destiny. The hard work started and ended with him.

There were no days off. He took complete responsibility for his life and was never afraid of a challenge. Chad saw the world through a beautiful lens, and he never lost hope— in Chad's life, HOPE always persevered.

Chad only knew how to live in the moment. He wasn't feeling sorry about what happened yesterday and wasn't lost in what could be tomorrow. Chad lived in the now. This unique ability to live in the moment gave rise to a life story that ended so beautifully that it amazingly overshadowed the pain and struggle that happened throughout.

Chad redefined excellence in his own way: showing the world that disability doesn't mean inability. He demonstrated to us through his actions that all of us have endless possibilities and everyone can live a successful, happy, and fulfilled life. Much like Chad, all persons with disabilities give us hope that if they can overcome obstacles despite a more difficult path, then surely we can too. Never underestimate the human spirit. Its strength alone can erase any obstacles.

I never heard Chad speak negatively about anyone other than the Dallas Cowboys, the Michigan State Spartans, and politicians — whether democrat or republican, who didn't embrace environmentalism. Chad was destined for greatness. Chad Hickman was an environmentalist. Chad knew right from wrong and would never waiver: to him the world was black and white. There was no grey. It was either right or wrong, and if it destroyed the earth or harmed a plant or an animal, no matter the cost, it was wrong. He understood the importance of nature and protecting our environment. He was talking about the importance of environmentalism before it even became a buzz word — before politicians and the media started talking global warming, Chad was talking conservation.

He composted, recycled, grew his own garden, and conserved water. He had greater character than any man I know. He wasn't influenced by popular opinion. Instead, he relied on his inner understanding of what was right for mankind and never gave in. He had a heart so big that he would be frustrated when a limb was cut from a tree. In his eyes, the tree was there before us, did nothing wrong, and most importantly, it provided us with the oxygen and shade that we need to live. To him, we are all one.

Chad was passionate and determined. He impacted the community because, like continually relearning to walk, Chad never gave up on anything or anyone.

Chad's ability to rise no matter the challenge gave a ubiquitous feeling of HOPE to an entire community that left us with the knowledge that we each have what it takes no matter the situation. I hear stories of Chad's inspiration on other's lives regularly, and if you mention Chad's name in his hometown of Fremont, Michigan, you just may hear about his influence. In Branstrom Park, a bridge has been erected named Chad Hickman's Bridge of Hope. It reads, "No matter our circumstances, Chad taught a community that HOPE always allows us to persevere."

Matthew Mansfield, who is a very close friend of Chad's, and a trusted confidant, friend, supporter, and listener, continues to remind his wife (and us) that if Chad could do it with his challenges, then we can too!

CHAPTER 1

Life Would Be Different Than Expected

I was born April 2, 1976. My Father, Terry, and my Mother, Jackie, were excited at the arrival of their second son. Amidst the chaos and excitement of a newborn, my parents found out that our lives were about to be changed forever.

My brother, Chad, was born 4 years earlier. They were young parents with little resources other than the love they had for each other and our Family, and their determination to give us a better life. Looking back, I'm sure my parents could've never imagined the journey they would be on.

The jubilation of a newborn son would quickly turn to fear as my brother was diagnosed with brain cancer and given a slim chance of survival. Technology had not caught up to where it's at today, so they were able to do surgery on one of the brain tumors and then they used radiation on the other tumor. Radiation treatment and scans were much different, so they targeted his brain and spinal column with large amounts of radiation. With great fortune, the radiation treatments saved his life, and then set into motion a sequence of life events that the best Hollywood director couldn't have scripted.

My Dad worked for a local grocery store and my Mother cared for us. Tears will forever well up inside of me as I recall my Dad telling me the story of his work insisting that he return to work full time or quit to take care of my very sick brother. My young mother was left to care for a young baby and navigate my brother's battle with cancer.

Mom would bring Chad and I to the hospital for his 45 radiation treatments. We lived an hour or so from the main hospital, so we would get Chad's blood taken in our hometown hospital, and after finding out if his levels were ok, we would drive south to Grand Rapids. The local hospital was a few blocks away from my parent's house and my Mom would sit me next to Chad in the wheelchair and push us to the hospital. He couldn't walk and was such a sick young boy.

I doubt my Mom and Dad ever imagined, in the midst of this chaos, that this experience would begin to form an inseparable bond between their two sons filled with inspiration, respect, unconditional love, and most importantly, that our lives would be enhanced significantly from the experience.

I'm not sure that I'll ever be able to understand how my parents managed the challenges. It hadn't been until after Chad's passing that I honestly sat and thought of it.

As a result of the brain tumors and radiation, Chad had grand mal seizures, learning disabilities, had stunted growth (he had a 6-foot frame in a 4-foot 11-inch body), and had physical limitations. Most frustrating to him, though, was that his hair never grew back.

He always wore a hat and was known for his University of Michigan Wolverines hat. My Grandfather taught him to show respect though, so he always took his hat off at the table.

CHAPTER 2

To Me, The Familiar Was Not Unique

When I was growing up with Chad I didn't see my brother as unique. One of the stories that I told in his eulogy is that I'm really proud of how my parents handled the challenging situation because they gave him freedom and flexibility to live his life.

I remember they would send us to school on the bus every day. The bus stop was a quarter mile or so from our house down a long dirt road. We lived in the middle of 40 acres. I remember one instance vividly. We were getting off the bus one afternoon and Chad looked at me and said, "I know a shortcut." At this time in my life, I was not aware of Chad having any disabilities, so without hesitation I followed his lead. He ended up getting us lost but Dad came looking for us.

I can still see the path we took: the green ferns, the dirt two-track, and I can hear the leaves on the ground, crinkling beneath our feet. Those 40 acres were magical as a child and I'm grateful that my parents had the innocence to allow us the freedom to wander. Until now, I hadn't thought of what it was like for me to see Chad as my big brother. Later, roles seemed to be reversed as I cared for Chad and he looked to me for help.

But the day we got lost, Chad, my hero, lead us on a journey through the woods and I was none the wiser. Reflecting on this, the only real challenge Chad and I ever had in our relationship was his frustration from the perception that he wasn't the older brother. I'm sure that must have been challenging for him.

My parents gave Chad the perfect life because throughout his childhood he did not have many limitations. The beauty of his life was that they didn't put him in a little bubble to protect him — instead he had full range to live a beautiful life. I'm not sure if my parents intentionally gave him freedom or if they were innocent enough yet that they never realized to limit him. No matter, it worked out well.

I remember playing tackle football with him in the yard and in the hallway by our bedrooms. **During one game of** "hallway football," I broke Chad's finger. I didn't think Mom knew what had happened but, now, I have a hunch.

This makes me think of Chad's strong character and his respect for our relationship. I don't ever remember him tattling to my parents on me and I'm sure I gave him plenty of reasons to do so.

When we were younger, our Grandfather had gotten the Grandkids a three-wheeler and so Chad rode it. I remember one time he had a seizure and was thrown over the handle bars and the three-wheeler rolled over on him. He had marks on his head, but my parents just dusted him off and we went back to life. The focus wasn't on protecting Chad. Instead, he was allowed to live his life. This set the foundation for him having his freedom, and safety to live such a powerful and inspirational life.

CHAPTER 3

Finding His Voice

Chad was a slow learner as a result of the damage from the radiation. He was in a special education classroom in his elementary school years. The teachers and support he received from this experience were profound.

He had a teacher, Mr. Mooy, **who had a special influence on Chad.** John Mooy is now a professional storyteller and he spoke at Chad's Celebration of Life Ceremony. He was a remarkable connection for Chad to have had at that point in time. His influence would span three decades and my home is full of treasures from their relationship.

Mr. Mooy is a poet, writer, artist, and very creative. He has a cousin, Tony Angel, who is an artist. He was drawing a picture of a harbor seal which was **going to be part of a book.** Mr. Mooy wanted to get his class involved in a project as a way to bolster self-confidence. He wanted the students to redraw a small section of the harbor seal from their perspective and then they would put all of the pieces together to form their own version of the seal.

The thought was that each student in the classroom would draw one section of the seal on 8 ½ by 11 paper, and then they would connect them all together. It turned into a much larger project than Mr. Mooy ever expected.

The kids had a great time drawing the sections and when they went to put the picture up, they realized it was so large that they had to get ladders out and hang this replication on the gym wall.

This project helped the teachers and my parents understand Chad's determination **when challenged to do something.** This determination followed him through his amazing life and was the source of inspiration for our family, friends, community, and most importantly in aiding Chad's ability to create the best possible life given his situation.

The following story I learned at Chad's Celebration of Life and I will never forget it.

Mr. Mooy had also written a long poem to go with the harbor seal drawing. It was over a page in length. Not expecting someone to take the bait, John went to all the kids and said that if you can recite this poem I'll take you to lunch. At the memorial, John shared that Chad came into his office well after the project's completion and said, "I'm ready!"

Mr. Mooy said, "Ready, ready for what?"

Chad said, "I can recite the poem."

"What poem?" stated Mr. Mooy? He had completely lost track of the challenge. Chad then recited the entire poem. John had later talked to my Mom, and I guess Chad had about driven my mother crazy with the poem because he spent so much time trying to memorize the piece. When he had something in his mind, he was determined to make it happen.

This story helps me understand the pride he had in himself to believe he was capable. I smile of Chad thinking, "Hey, I know you didn't expect me to do this but here it is."

Another thing that Mr. Mooy did that was really profound in Chad's life is that as a class, they would write to professional sport athletes. The letter would start out with...Dear..., I am writing to people I like and admire.... and then he would ask them for an autograph. This was in the 80's and pre-eBay, so nearly everyone sent back a signed photograph. Chad had a house full of these treasures. He has signatures from All-stars like Al Kaline, Kirby Puckett, Nolan Ryan, Johnny Bench, and Rickey Henderson.

His collection is impressive. He had people like the famed Coach Tommy Lasorda writing: "To Chad – a future Dodger. God Bless you. Your friend, Tom!" Or "Dear Chad," ... I personally saved any that had Chad's name on them. It was at a time when people would be very personal about what they wrote with the autograph. He had amassed quite a collection. Later on, my Dad had them all framed, and after Chad passed away, we spread the autographs throughout the family for everyone to enjoy.

The uniqueness is that Chad continued to write to people he liked and admired throughout his life. Unfortunately, with the creation of eBay, he didn't really get anything in return, but he still wrote them. One of my cherished pieces is a letter from Dave Dombrowski, the former General Manager of the Detroit Tigers. Chad had written him about a player, Pudge Rodriguez. Chad didn't like the trade that was made, so Dave Dombrowski wrote back to him and offered some insight into why he had made that trade.

This experience turned into something that gave Chad a powerful voice. He started out writing innocent requests for autographs and it became him vocalizing concerns he had in the world. He would write coaches on Monday if he was unhappy with a game that weekend and gave his two cents on what he would do. This was really important because it allowed Chad to find his voice.

Chad wrote his thoughts in pencil to athletes, companies, and politicians for over three decades. He would even make his own envelope by taking an 8 ½ by 11 paper and he would fold it, tape it, and staple it. I still have the letter template that he used to write all his letters. It isn't in its original form, but the words were the same John Mooy taught him over three decades earlier.

Chad's most cherished piece is a response to a letter he wrote in the early 90's to Terry Bradshaw, former famed Quarterback for the Pittsburgh Steelers, and asked for his autograph. My Dad included a video of Chad's impressive autograph collection and he talked about how he really admired Terry Bradshaw. In the video he asked, "If I send you a football, a helmet and a jersey will you sign it?" Terry Bradshaw received the letter and replied with a yes. Those items became Chad's most prized possessions.

As Chad continued to find confidence in sharing his voice, he would later write to companies. If the company had products that weren't recyclable, he would write a letter asking them to consider using recyclable materials.

Chadism: He was frustrated with the disposable society and never used a paper plate, paper napkin, or plasticware, so my Mother used cloth napkins for him.

Chad was a champion for animal rights and environmentalism. He would write local politicians, our Mayor, the Governor, and our State Legislators, and expressed his concerns about these topics. It usually had to do with how to deal with animal rights or environmental policy.

Chad wasn't just vocal in the community. Chad's voice reached well beyond the Fremont area. President Obama wrote a letter to him in response to Chad's thoughts on his environmental policy. The President wrote, "Thank you for writing. I have heard from many Americans concerned about environmental issues, from recycling and pollution control to the well-being of our national parks and wildlife. I appreciate your perspective." I have the letter framed in my office.

Chad took action, didn't pass on the responsibility, or assume the work would get done by others. He used his voice to try to make change. Chad taught us all, that one person can make a difference. Chad's life was far from perfect, but he lived it with perfection. He lived every moment with intention, purpose, and accepting life as it was and not how it should be. Imagine if all of us followed in his footsteps.

CHAPTER 4

Environmentalism Became His Passion

Chad was ahead of his time. He was always an environmentalist. He was talking recycling and conservation long before those ideas were spoken of in the mainstream.

He worked for Fremont Area Recycle Center and the Director taught him about recycling decades ago. This became his lifelong passion and as I speak of Chad's life, I always mention that he was an environmentalist.

The unique thing is that this all happened organically and was done completely on his own. We didn't have recycling in the home and recycling was not something that was even talked about. This was back in the early nineties, before recycling became more of a buzzword. Chad started having conversations and got really, really demanding that we as a family and as a business have better recycling practices.

He ended his work for the Fremont Recycle Center only because in the wintertime it just got to be too cold because the facility didn't have heat. This led Chad to recycling around the house and then in our Family business.

In my parent's house in Fremont, Michigan, my Dad had an extra stall in the garage and he set up a recycling center for Chad. He would recycle everything around the house and then word got around to the neighborhood. Soon, all the neighbors started bringing their recyclables over to Chad. They would bring the recycling in a crate and then Chad would sort it into bins. My Dad would take him every Saturday to the local recycling center where Chad would deposit each of the hundreds of items into the appropriate recycle bin.

Environmentalism became a huge part of Chad's life as it morphed into so much more when it turned into water preservation. He did not like using a lot of water and would struggle when my parents wanted to use water or if he had to wash his hands and dishes because he *really* didn't want to waste water. He knew years ago that water was a precious resource.

Chadism: Chad never emptied a glass of water in the sink. Instead, he would leave the glass on the counter and continue to refill it. Chad never drank a plastic bottle of water.

Chad also composted. He had a drum barrel composter and he composted everything. Basically, with Chad in the house, my parents never had any trash.

He cut up paper towels, saved finger nail clippings and beard trimmings from the shaver and composted them.

He also grew a garden, so his compost would be used in the garden every year. My Dad, bless his commitment and patience, set up an area in the yard for Chad's garden, complete with a sprinkling system and fencing to keep animals away. And bless my Mother. She would help till, plant, and weed.

While he was still in good health, Chad and our Grandfather would go and get seeds and plants together in the spring. Doing so was a very **special experience for the two of them.** My Grandfather was Chad's influence and mentor in gardening and in life.

Many of the things Chad grew, he didn't eat, like the tomatoes. Instead, he gave the vegetables to everybody. He enjoyed giving the produce away. He would grow cucumbers, leaf lettuce, carrots, and even purple potatoes. He liked the different colored potatoes best. I believe he saw his produce like he saw life — that our differences make us better. Chad's garden was a huge passion of his.

Chad may have been challenged with mental and physical limitations, but he was gifted with patience, determination, and the ability to live completely in the moment. No matter his struggles in life, Chad found peace in the routine of everyday life and didn't bounce between the regret of yesterday or anxiety of tomorrow. His ability to live in the moment gave him super powers.

Chadism: He had so much patience that he played penny slots - one penny at a time.

CHAPTER 5

One Person Can Make A Difference

Chad was given the same opportunities as every young man should. As young boys, with our friend Chris, we started a business with the help of my Dad. Our company was called CNC Novelties, which stood for the three friends: Chad, Nathan, and Chris. We were like the three little pigs, always together.

We sold engravings that had quotes or phrases on them. The plastic engraved pieces sat on a wooden base to be placed on a desk. We would take the wood, **cut it to shape,** put a slot in it so the plastic piece could sit in it and hold it up. Then we would stain the base. That was our little company.

Then we sold the signs to local gas stations. The stations would put it on their counter. We also put the Engraved Novelty Signs in baggies and hung them on a tree type stand that we built. This was our first glimpse into entrepreneurship and we continued to work together for 25+ years.

Chad's favorite quote was "Life doesn't suck, it's just not fair." Little did I know at the time that Chad had the answer to the complexity of life even way back then.

In the late nineties my parents moved Show & Tell Demonstration Service, the Family business my Mom and Dad started back in 1978, to the Fremont, Michigan, industrial park. It had outgrown the home and the garage. We built a warehouse and office facility in the industrial park with the intent of having some warehouse space.

Gerber Baby Food was founded and located in Fremont, and they had found out that we had some warehouse space and they had a unique need that we filled: **repackaging products as promotional materials.** It later morphed into a nice business, so we decide to use the name CNC and it became CNC National Enterprises.

This is where Chad started bailing cardboard. He took baby food boxes and bailed the cardboard. He had his own bailer and knew how to do all the processes. Our employees put the boxes in carts and would send them over his way. For 6 hours a day, he would throw the boxes into a bailer and this gave him significant quality of life. Everyone would go on break and Chad kept bailing away. This was Chad's lifeblood. He was proud of CNC.

Over the years we had a number of employees anywhere from a couple dozen to fifty or seventy-five at a time. Chad related well with everyone and had great personal connections with the staff. They had all the respect in the world for him.

I really never met anybody in my life that didn't respect Chad. He had an aura of respect around him, and when he came into the room, he commanded the room. He had this great presence and I still feel like he has that presence today. What he did was really special. If people were using profanity or people were being disrespectful, they usually had enough respect for Chad that even the tone of the conversations would change.

It was almost like how you would communicate around your grandfather or someone of that level. The respect came from his confidence and his willingness to stand up for himself and for what was right.

He may have been short in stature, thought of as a young boy, and mostly missing hair, but he never backed down and he earned respect from everyone. He had confidence and a kind demeanor and people understood his determination to succeed. It gave him credibility.

Chad bailed about 2 million pounds of cardboard over the course of his career with our Family business, CNC National Enterprises. We had so much cardboard that Chad bailed it 6 hours a day. **He would come into the office and lay his service dog, Gable, in the air-conditioned break room — he wanted Gable to stay comfortable and clean. Then he would put on his knife-holster and get to work.**

To put the 2 million pounds (1,000 tons) of cardboard Chad recycled into perspective, recycling one ton of cardboard saves about 390 kWh of energy based on Waste Management's website. And based on the average annual electricity consumption for a U.S. residential utility customer (by the 2016 US Energy Information Administration,) Chad's recycling could power your home for 36 years.

In August 2013 in The Herald News, Margaret Kemp's article "Recycling Cardboard: A Never- Ending Task" mentions that recycling one ton of cardboard saves over 9 cubic yards of landfill space. Based on the average body size of a garbage truck by Prince Motor USA, Chad's efforts saved up to 225 truckloads of trash from going to our local landfill. Chad proved that one person can make a difference.

After he was done bailing cardboard, he would go around to each of the trash cans in the office and make sure that everyone was recycling their office paper and meal containers. If you had not recycled to his liking, he would write you a note...in pencil, and put it on your desk. He would, basically, in a nice way, ask you to change your behavior. Everyone had a ton of respect for Chad, so he usually didn't have to write multiple notes.

Looking back with shame, our very close friend Chris McClure and I fought Chad on his recycling efforts. I think Chad grumbled quite a bit because he had to write us many notes over the years, but he would be proud now because his influence has been profound.

Chris is now the VP and General Manager for a company out of Illinois and he set up a recycling program for his company. Because he lives in Illinois and they don't have bottle deposit, he also communicates with owners of bars and restaurants, and tries to get them to find a better way to recycle their glass and cans instead of throwing them in the trash. Chad was able to get many in the community excited about recycling and involved in it.

Chad worked 5 days a week through pain that would have debilitated most of us. He lived with my parents and he would get ready in the morning and call the office and have my Dad or me go pick him up. My parents only lived a couple miles from the office; we would bring him in and he would start his day. We didn't want him to feel rushed to have to be there at a certain time. He had a strict routine to get ready in the morning. Mornings were a huge part of his life. Chad was routine oriented and everything he did was the same nearly every day. It was that way for his entire life.

Reflecting on this morning routine, I see his wisdom in not starting the day rushed and hurried. If we travelled and had to catch an early flight, he would get up early enough, so he could still get his routine in. This routine brought balance and consistency to what would become ever-changing health challenges. It brought him stability and peace.

I took a page out of his playbook and instituted this practice into my life. I'm a night owl — I wrote this entire book on my phone in the middle of the night — so most of my life I got up with minutes to spare, rushed out the door without eating, and would hope to make a 20-minute trip to work in 18 minutes. This would cause me to start my day negatively and often I wouldn't recover all day, and I absolutely hated mornings.

After reflecting on Chad's wisdom, I shifted my day a few hours, so I don't start my day until after 10 am. This allows me to get up without an alarm clock, eat, read, sometimes lie back down and then start my day peacefully. I started embracing that a one-size-fits-all approach doesn't work for everyone and began to take control of areas where I had struggled for so long — like my hatred of mornings.

CHAPTER 6

Inspiring Connections

Chad always made unique connections. No one ever forgot him. In the fall, Show & Tell would work a special event at the DeVos Place Convention Center in Grand Rapids, which was the Grand Center at the time. Every year, the weekend after Labor Day, the city of Grand Rapids held "Celebration on the Grand," and Meijer (a local grocery store) would have a food fair. Meijer would take up the whole Grand Center and they would have their vendors come in. You would pay a small fee and then you would get to sample food or receive free items from these vendors.

It was a great and fun event. Show & Tell would bring in a couple hundred workers to help the vendors. It turned into a fun event for us and we would pay all of our best employees from all over the Midwest to come to the Grand Center. We housed them and recognized them for their efforts from the previous year.

This is where Chad connected with Margaret Anisko. She was a demonstrator that worked for us for many years and Margaret was a special lady. She was paired up in a vendor booth with Chad where they handed out samples.

She had so much love and respect for Chad that she insisted they work together every year and she became a Grandmother figure to him. She would write him letters and send him cards on his birthday and Christmas, but they had not gotten together in a while. The fall before Chad passed away, I wanted to get Margaret and Chad together. The meeting between the two was magical to watch.

A woman in her 90's, who had seen so much over her lifetime, including the loss of her beloved husband, was enamored with Chad. She had so much respect for the way he lived his life, how he managed tragedy and how he still pressed on without complaint. She held his hand during the visit and he obliged even though he mostly stayed away from touching people. They both had respect for the way they endured the battles of life. It was remarkable to see this woman's admiration for him. Chad, throughout the years, had given *her* HOPE!

CHAPTER 7

Another Setback

Adding to the complexity of his cancer diagnose and subsequent treatments and surgery, Chad developed grand mal seizures. He had no inclination that he would be having one, and he would completely black out and lose consciousness, falling immediately to the ground from whatever position he was in. Even though he had seizures, my parents didn't limit his life. He swam in the Muskegon River, went to school on his own, and had a fair amount of independence.

Then in 1994, Chad's life changed dramatically. I was a senior at Grant High School and in Mr. Stickney's Government class taking a test that fateful day. I still remember where I was sitting and who was in front of me. My parents were in Hawaii and a cousin was staying with Chad and me.

During the test, I had gotten a phone call at the school office. I had to rush home to my brother because he had a seizure and fell. He hit his head on the concrete and had a hematoma. When I got home he was unconscious, vomiting, and the paramedics were getting him on the stretcher.

They rushed him to the community hospital and then on to Grand Rapids. My parents were in Hawaii and at least a day away from being able to arrive. Decisions were made over the phone and Chad was rushed into surgery. Someone asked what I needed, and I instantly asked for my best friend Chris. His Mom got him out of school and we went to the hospital nearly an hour away.

I remember the staff asking if we wanted to have his whole head shaved or just half. All I could think about was his hair and how he would feel with it gone. Chad's hair, or lack of, was always a sore spot for him.

We spent the night in the hospital. My aunts, Chris, and cousin all stayed in the lobby. I remember the first time I was able to go into his room after surgery. He was in ICU — I didn't even know what that meant — and he was hooked up to so many machines and tubes and wires. I still hear the beeping of the machines. The anxiety of not knowing, the lack of control over the outcome, and that beeping sound would become a regular part of our life. I slept in Chad's ICU room in a chair next to him and held his hand.

My parents arrived the next day and then over the next few days I tried to resume "life." Weeks later, Mr. Stickney had an opportunity to take our class to Muskegon Community College for his Government class. We were practicing labor negotiations. Stick knew my thoughts on the topic and assigned me to the opposing team.

As we were getting ready to start, Stick came and got me from the event. He said, "Your neighbors are picking you up. It's your brother, you have to leave now." I vaguely recall where we were on campus, but I can feel the cold air and remember being in my neighbor's truck. The rest is fuzzy.

When I arrived at the hospital I remember seeing my parents. Chad had gone into convulsions and wasn't coming out. They were concerned about brain damage — they thought he might die. What crossed my mind at that moment is: *How did my parents find me; how did my neighbors know where to go and how did my parents find the courage and willpower to arrange all that.* Chad was in critical condition and yet, I was a priority.

While in the hospital in Grand Rapids, Chad's room partner was a Detroit Lion. One day, my Dad was outside the hospital and a limo pulled up. Lomas Brown, a Detroit Lion, was visiting his teammate. Chad had the opportunity to meet Lomas and even he was impressed by Chad's determination and resilience. Later Chad received a signed card by Lomas Brown, Barry Sanders, and the team mascot, Huddles that read, "We're cheering for you!"

Chad was a determined young man and he pulled through but not without sacrifice. He couldn't walk, he couldn't eat, and he had to relearn life. But that never stopped Chad. I don't ever remember him complaining or feeling sorry for himself. He went to a rehab hospital and slowly pressed on with a commanding determination to succeed no matter what the new norm would become.

He did learn to walk but this time the biggest setback was his loss of independence. We no longer could let him be alone — another fall could kill him.

My parents worked with Paws with A Cause and Chad became a pet parent to a service dog that could sense seizures and also get help. There was a bell in the bathroom, for example, and the dog gave us some sense of relief as Chad went on with his life. Unfortunately, this meant that Chad lost his dignity from that point on. He could seize at any time and would then have to be saved from seizing in the shower or on the toilet.

Our family talks of the importance of our friend Chris McClure. Chris spent most of his free time with us. He had a sixth sense and when Chad seized, we would find him running, jumping, and even diving to catch him to break the fall. Their connection was special. Although technically not brothers, they filled that role in each other's lives.

After several seizures, Chad had to start wearing a helmet. Not having hair bothered him, and he certainly did not like the helmet. He rarely showed frustration as he was even tempered and largely calm, but that helmet drove him crazy. He knew people looked at him differently. He was already shorter than most, looked different, and now stood out wearing a helmet.

This never stopped him though. We lived life and went to concerts, sporting events, and movies. You may think this would've broken Chad's spirit, but it was quite the contrary. He became stronger, more determined, more resilient, and our connection would strengthen and our respect for each other grew immensely. Our family unit was challenged, and we got closer.

In Chad's life hope always persevered. That's the reason he had such great quality of life and why he was able to do such special things. He never lost hope. As matter fact, in his eulogy, I said, "Chad had an inability to lose hope!" It was never "why me?" or "why can't I?" or "poor me!" It was always: "What do I have to do to get to the next step?"

CHAPTER 8

Reclaiming Independence

My parents were excellent advocates for my brother. Their strong, determined personalities were a big reason why Chad had great quality of life. Chad lived with my parents and they managed every aspect of his life to ensure his health; however, they didn't control it. My parents concern after the hematoma in 1994, and the subsequent increase in seizure activity, left them feeling that the next fall may take his life.

They researched a surgery that would remove the portion of the brain with seizure activity. This was before the internet was within everyone's reach. They started working with Henry Ford Hospital in Detroit. The testing was extensive as the doctors needed to know what part of the brain caused the seizure activity, and since it was going to be removed, they needed to know its function so that Chad would not be incapacitated.

Chad ended up having the surgery at Cleveland Clinic in Ohio. This was a scary experience. We travelled as a family, along with Chris, to Cleveland and we stayed there for a week.

The surgery was incredibly successful. Dr. Bingaman will forever be remembered as the person who gave Chad his life back. He is my hero. It took time for Chad to heal and it took more time for our family to regain trust that Chad would not seize — but Chad never had a grand mal seizure again. He was able to retire his helmet.

It is during this week at Cleveland Clinic that Chad met an incredibly influential person. Dr. Peggy Crawford was assigned to Chad as a psychotherapist to help him emotionally get through the hemispherectomy surgery. They connected instantly; however, she practiced in Ohio and Chad lived in Michigan. Health insurance wouldn't pay for ongoing visits, so Dr. Crawford called Chad on Saturday afternoons during her free time to talk with him. She did this for more than a decade and they formed a tight bond. Chad became friends with Peggy and her husband Dennis. They would even come up to Michigan to visit Chad.

Peggy documented every call for more than a decade and has a filing cabinet full of Chad's stories or as she calls them "Chadisms." To Peggy, "Chadisms" are those unique beliefs that allowed him to overcome obstacles. Over the years Chad had as much impact on her and Dennis as they did on him. She would listen to Chad's stories and they had an influence on her. She began working out regularly after hearing Chad talk about his physical therapy, and exercise became a part of her life.

Chad's impact on others was profound. He inspired people to be a better version on themselves and he gave us all hope that by working hard you can achieve more than you ever expected.

After the surgery, Chad began to get his independence back. My parents would leave him alone in the home for a few hours at a time. He made breakfast and lunch for himself and when I stayed overnight with him, he made us both dinner. Chad enjoyed taking care of little brother Nathan. He was my biggest fan, but it did irritate him that I didn't cook. The only time he was hard on me was when I wasn't doing the things he felt I should to maintain a healthy lifestyle.

Chadism: Chad always put fresh berries on his breakfast Cheerios and he never skipped breakfast, lunch, or dinner.

My Dad and Chad bowled on a league, and every Friday night they would take lessons. The bowling community in Fremont treated Chad with such dignity and respect. It was a big part of his life. Chad loved sports, and given his physical limitations, bowling became the sport that he could excel at. After years of practice he was hard to beat, and their team won the league one year – they actually went from dead last in previous years to first place.

I stayed with him often in the summer, so my parents had a chance to get away. Chad and I would go to movies and concerts and had a great time together. When we would go shopping for groceries, it became a lesson in patience for me. I went from making decisions in the store for him to understanding the value of the experience for Chad. He had trouble making decisions and I learned to allow him the space to make choices under his terms. We could spend a half hour in the cereal or chip aisle.

Looking back, these opportunities to stay with Chad not only solidified our bond, but it also gave him purpose. I didn't mind him taking care of me, so he would cook dinner, take care of the cat, and vacuum the floors.

Chadism: Chad never ate fast food, never drank a full can of pop, and always ate at the table.

Concerts, movies, and dinner at a restaurant were his favorite activities with me. We probably went to 50 + concerts. Some of the bands I would take him to see were his favorites and I went to give him the experience. Often these bands would become my favorite. Styx is one of those bands. Chad absolutely loved 60's and 70's classic rock. Styx was playing locally one year, and I took him to the show. This became "our band" and one of my all-time favorite concerts to go to. I always think of Chad when "Come Sail Away" by Styx comes on.

Chad was normally shy, but at concerts he would get lost in the emotion. He stood throughout the concert, raised his arm, pumped his fist, and belted the words. He wasn't bashful in that environment. He also listened to music during his long morning routine. He jammed to music and sang every morning.

Our bond grew through these experiences and through sports. We followed the same sporting teams — well, actually I followed them for him — and learned to enjoy them. There were years where Chad and I would watch the entire NFL draft. He was a die-hard Detroit Lions fan and he had hope every year that the new draft class would bring a championship to Detroit.

My Dad and Chad bonded through sports also and so did many of Chad's other friends. He would text from his iPad throughout a game with scoring updates and his thoughts on the game. These became important connections for us.

For over a decade after the brain surgery to stop the seizures, Chad found himself having more independence than he ever had. Life was almost normal.

CHAPTER 9

Independence May Be Lost But Not His Determination or Spirit

In 2012, Chad had a stroke. It was a Sunday morning when my Dad called. Sundays are my day of rest and are usually the only day I don't speak with my parents. They especially know I love to sleep in so a phone call early on a Sunday gave me instant anxiety. I knew something was wrong.

When I answered the phone, I heard my Dad say, "Nathan, your brother had a stroke." Chad had been at the community hospital with stroke symptoms and they were transferring him to the main hospital for more care. Our family was in shock. We had enjoyed a relatively good period in terms of Chad's health. In the first hours we didn't know what had potentially been damaged by the stroke.

I was scared to see him lying on a stretcher at the hospital. We had so many questions and so many worries, and as you may imagine, it took time to sort out.

The first few days I was nearly paralyzed with anxiety. My brain went to the worst as it had been conditioned to over the years with Chad's health struggles. I felt lost in the unknown.

Fortunately, we found out that any significant damage done by the stroke was only to his right side. He couldn't use his right arm, hand, or leg. We were relieved that cognitively he was unharmed. He stayed in the hospital for a few weeks and was transferred to a rehab hospital.

I worked a blended second shift for a local company, so I could come over every night and have dinner with Chad and my parents.

In a state of flux and concern, I was surprised when my boss reached out and said, "Nathan, there's work to be done." My nerves were shot from the anxiousness of the unknown and this felt all too familiar to my Dad being asked by his boss to choose between work and my brother's care when he was diagnosed as a young boy. It ended up being a blessing because I left that organization and it allowed me time with my brother.

I had always been the backup for my parents. They cared for Chad day in and day out and were proud and happy to do so, but they needed relief. I was the primary caregiver after them. I'm grateful that I had the freedom to be part of Chad's recovery.

This stroke was a setback for sure, but it felt more difficult for my parents and myself than it did for Chad. Chad was ready to start rehab the moment he was hospitalized. He didn't worry about not using his arm or leg because he didn't doubt that he would recover. This was his third time learning to walk and the third time is always the charm as they say.

He learned to walk again but ended up needing a walker for stability. As a family we hurt for Chad. He had finally gotten some freedom and independence after his surgery and now — he was back to square one. He needed help with every aspect of living.

Luckily, my parents, around a decade earlier, had the foresight that Chad wasn't going to live a normal life. When they built a new home, they made it barrier-free so that he would be able to live at home no matter the circumstance.

He received physical therapy, worked at home on his own, and had a physical trainer. His support team was phenomenal as not only did they encourage him, but I think they also were inspired by Chad.

For physical therapy and training, Chad attended The Tamarac, an affiliate of Spectrum Health. His team worked tirelessly to give him the best quality of life possible. It was an excellent community for him because in that setting, he was seen as a hero and not as disabled. He overcame challenges where most would've thrown in the towel. The Tamarac and those in the community of Fremont, Michigan, saw Chad as strong and determined. They were proud of him and never made him feel different in any way.

Chad was so regarded at The Tamarac that he once was runner up for Citizen of the Year. He worked hard to regain some of what he had lost. He was probably one of the best patients a doctor ever could have, because whatever the doctor said, it was done that way. Chad made sure of that.

When I speak of Chad inspiring a community, it's the community of Fremont. Fremont was so special to Chad. The people in Fremont supported and encouraged him in ways which they may not realize.

In the late nineties, we had plans on moving the business and our home to Grand Rapids, but we knew that the community was perfect for Chad and it gave him amazing quality of life — beyond what we could've imagined.

He didn't let this setback keep him from fulfilling his passion. The neighbors still brought over their recycling, and with his walker near him, he would sort the recyclables. My Dad also put pots in the driveway so that Chad could still grow his garden.

Chad found ways to keep his mind focused away from the negativity. He didn't think in terms of what he couldn't do and never focused on what was wrong. His focus and determination were on what he could do in the moment.

He was mentally slow in terms of traditional education, but Chad was as mentally tough as a Navy Seal. He tricked his brain by focusing on what he did have and on what he could do and never discussed what had happened or what may happen. He figured life out. His ability to focus on this moment saved his life from pain, anger, and discontent.

He had learned to use heat and cold packs as well as meditation to ease his significant physical pain. He lived most of his life in unimaginable pain but most of the world would never know how bad it really was. He took nearly 300 OxyContin pills every month and it barely masked the pain. Chad pushed on — never showing weakness. He taught himself resilience and this is how he coped every day. To help understand some of Chad's tremendous pain, he had a 6-foot-tall skeleton in a 4-foot 11-inch body. Coupled with the years of brain injury and trauma, he had little relief.

Chad lived a very structured life and it was also a significant reason why he had such a great quality of life despite everything. He woke up nearly the same time each day, worked really hard at getting showered and shaved, and ate a healthy breakfast. He made his own breakfast and would walk it from the kitchen counter to the table. It was a pleasure watching him walk some around the house without his walker. Chad needed independence and he needed to have hope. Although most days were hard on his body, he showered and shaved every day. Many of us struggle with this under normal conditions.

Chadism: Chad didn't like the simplicity of microwaves and never used one to heat meals – other than popcorn.

Chad knew he needed to start his day off as if it was going to be a success. Every day Chad had purpose and he found meaning. He only watched TV a little in the morning and at night. During the day he worked hard at living life. He never napped unless he had severe head pain. He was hopeful that if he worked hard every day, each day would be better. He NEVER procrastinated. I know I could benefit from this determination.

Chadism: Chad went to bed and woke up at the same time every day.

CHAPTER 10

Giving Up Is Not an Option

We slowly got used to life with Chad and his walker. He was working with personal trainers every day, doing exercises on his own and he had found a rhythm to life. His day was slowed down because of the time it took to do tasks, but he was doing most things on his own.

That fall I flew Chad to Naples, Florida, to meet up with my parents. They live there in the winter. My parents drive down, but that trip would've been excruciatingly painful for Chad.

I'll never forget the day we flew. We left early in the morning and I set an alarm to wake up Chad. When I woke up, he was already ready and waiting for me. He had gotten himself up at around 1 am to give himself time for his full morning routine.

I was so proud of Chad that day. I wheeled him in a wheelchair through the airport and into the jet bridge, but he walked into the plane and to his seat by himself. His face was focused with determination as he took each step.

While in Florida, Styx and REO Speedwagon were having a concert in the nearby town. Chad and I always enjoyed music, so we went to the concert. We sat in handicap seating. I remember the parents of a special-needs son sitting next to us. He was completely paralyzed.

Waiting for the first band, I was in awe of what the parents were doing for their boy. The amount of work to get him in the arena and to keep him comfortable was phenomenal. In that moment I felt blessed. Chad may have had struggles, but he was still a lucky one.

Unfortunately, we left right after the first band took the stage. Chad was in significant pain. I drove him home and was sad knowing that certain parts of our lives would never be the same. After I dropped Chad off at home, I returned to the arena. The staff were gracious and let me back in. Styx was our band. We had watched them several times before and Chad and I loved watching them perform. They put on a show that is larger than life. Much like what Chad was able to do with his life. I knew he would be disappointed that I missed part of the show because of him.

After the Thanksgiving holiday Chad stayed in Florida, and I returned home to Grand Rapids. I started to get into the holiday spirit and back to my routine.

Then on a late afternoon I received a phone call from my parents. I specifically remember sitting in my home office printing a document when the desk vibrated. I expected to hear a hello from my Mother and was surprised when I heard my Dad on the other end. Dad said, "Nathan, your brother has pneumonia. Maybe you should come to Florida." He had been sick for some time and much like when he was a toddler, the doctors felt his ailments were from upper respiratory infections. At the time, they had no idea of the extent of what was going to happen.

Since my Dad was buying the ticket, I felt guilty of the cost because I could only get a first-class seat on the plane that left the next morning. When I boarded the plane, I had the whole first row to myself. It was surreal. I felt like I was the only one on the plane.

As the plane took off, I was listening to music through headphones when the song "Come Sail Away" by Styx came on. Tears came from seemingly nowhere. In that moment I knew something in our lives was about to change. I listened to the song over and over as I thought about Chad's life — cancer as a young boy, seizures, brain injury, brain surgery, and just the year prior: a stroke. I was mad. I was thinking *Chad doesn't deserve this life.* He is an amazing person. Why does Chad have to continue to struggle? Why? Why?

When I saw Chad in the hospital, he looked so sick. It wasn't the Chad I had seen when I left after Thanksgiving.

The doctor asked to talk to my parents and me. I can still see where we were sitting. I still feel the atmosphere in the room, and I still see my parents. That afternoon he had been diagnosed with lung cancer. We had no idea how bad the situation was. Chad was a fighter and we were all ready to put on our gloves.

As the doctors did more tests they found that he also had cancer in his bones and that his hip was nearly broken because of the cancer. He had surgery and they put a rod in his hip to prevent a complete break. We knew that Chad never lost hope and that we weren't going to take that from him. If Chad hadn't had surgery, he would've been confined to a bed. We knew that this wasn't what Chad would want. After the surgery Chad quickly went into determination mode. He was focused on walking again.

Against the odds, he ended up learning to walk one last time — he took 19 steps. My dad proudly counted every one of them.

Chad had always bounced back from a challenge, so we remained positive for him. We, too, had hope. Chad was the center of our world. We worked as a Family unit of Four. We did everything together. As Chad recovered from surgery and did rehab, we started to plan for what was next, as we always had done.

The first night Chad was in the hospital, we left him alone overnight for the first time. My mother had always stayed at the hospital with him, but they only lived a few minutes away and we knew we were in for a long haul and wanted to be rested for Chad.

The next evening, I was talking to Chad before we were about to leave for the night. Chad teared up. He was scared, and I had never seen fear in him. The nurses from the night before weren't responsive to his needs and he was frightened. I knew then that we wouldn't leave him alone again. I stayed that night and took the night shift from then on. I would stay with Chad at night and in the morning, when my parents returned, I would go to their house to rest. It felt so good being with him. I was comforted in knowing that I could help. In the middle of the night, I would be dozing off in a chair and hear Chad say, "Nathan." That usually meant he needed to use the bathroom.

Over the course of many weeks, Chad found himself living another new norm and we were trying to get answers. From our understanding at the time, Chad's lung cancer had developed from a left-over cancer cell from 1976. It was incredibly rare for cancer to go from neurologic to systemic (from brain/nerves to soft tissue) and the doctors didn't know what to expect. We knew it was a matter of time, but we thought we had more moments to share.

Chad finally got to come home from the hospital. We had a hospital bed delivered and it was in our living room. Chad was only able to stay one night though. The pain was so severe. I woke up the next morning to my parents in panic. This was a new type of panic for me to see. Chad had been through so much and my parents pushed on every time. The end felt near.

In January of 2014, in the middle of a beautiful southwest Florida winter night, I sat beside my brother's bedside with my Mom and Dad. It ended up being one of the last nights we were all together. Chad was in a hospice home and lung cancer was aggressively taking him from us.

Sitting with him and my parents, an overwhelming emotion came over me as I held his warm, strong hand, looked into his closed eyes, and told him, "Chad, don't worry about us. Do what you need to do." He was incredibly determined, and I felt that he was holding on for us. At that moment, I found peace in my brother's passing. It was so comforting being away from the hospital with all the phones ringing, monitors endlessly chirping and the four of us being together, as we always were.

It would be a few more days before he took his last breath, but that moment will forever be in my mind. I had found peace because our family, although imperfect, had given Chad the perfect life. Chad seemingly always had significant health challenges, and even though many of the situations were dire, Chad had strength and determination. We only knew to fight and press on.

We had not left the Hospice Home for several days because we knew that the time was coming. We asked the director of the home what the progression was for Chad's end. We were confused because he kept holding on. She told us that he's a 40-year-old man, and that although he had a number of health challenges, he had a strong heart and a strong body. She mentioned it would take him longer to pass.

My Dad and I had decided to go back to their place and shower and rest. Before I left I went up to Chad's bedside. He was no longer able to speak or respond. I had no idea if he was conscious. I spoke to him and said how proud I was of him and how grateful I was for his love and what he had taught me. I told him: "Do what you have to do Chad." I expressed how much I loved him.

Then my Dad and I started back to the house. On our way there, Mom called us and said that Chad was having trouble breathing and that we may want to come back. By the time we arrived back at hospice, he had already passed. I remember being so frustrated. I was in shock. The first thing out of me was anger! Why was I not there when he died? I stormed off and went away from the family and just took some time to myself outside. My Dad later came and got me, so we could say our final goodbyes as a family.

My Mother with her unique knowledge said, "You know, maybe Chad felt comfortable to go at this time because he knew that you had left. You gave him permission to end his life. Chad lived his life for you. He was dedicated to you and thought about you every second of every day." He was holding on for me and thought this time of me not being there was the time for him to go.

Thinking back of Chad's experience near the end, I'm really proud of his strength, courage, and resolve. Despite all these setbacks, I still never heard him complain or feel sorry for himself. He did the only thing he knew how to do and that was push on with his commanding determination.

Chadism: Chad had such pride and respect that he would clean the sink and counter from his wheelchair at the Hospice Home after he brushed his teeth.

When he had passed, the one thing I had was peace of mind that nothing was left on the table. I felt completely comfortable that Chad loved me, he knew I loved him, and I knew what we were meant to be together. It gave me great peace that everything that needed to be said was said and that I had done all I could over his lifetime.

I was so grateful that my Mother had the wisdom nearly three decades earlier to continually remind my Dad and me to never have regrets. She was preparing us for this moment and it is the most significant gift I'll ever receive.

CHAPTER 11

Chad's Life Had Significant Purpose

I have many great memories with Chad. I'm happy we had 41 amazing years together. I would never judge how other people live their life, but I know people that have lived eighty years and haven't had the quality of life that Chad had. The impact he made on the community and our family is profound. In my opinion, everything that we have as a Family is a result of Chad.

My parents were both very young when Chad was born and were working regular jobs and trying to raise a family. Chad gave my parents the strength and the courage to say *we want something more for the Family*. And so, my Dad started Show & Tell with my Mom.

Show & Tell was an in-store product demonstration service. For a lot of years, my Dad worked full-time at a grocery store and also worked full-time for Show & Tell. Starting and creating this business was a critical part of our lives. The four of us spent the majority of our life together every day. We worked and played together. We had such a unique bond and I think Chad solidified our connection.

He gave us all the strength and the courage to persevere and we knew that we had to fight on. I feel like we owe everything to Chad. He was a miracle in so many ways.

Chad didn't have to cure cancer to change the world. Instead, Chad taught us how to live despite having cancer. By societal norms, Chad didn't have a paying job, a formal education, a car, a house, or a significant other, but he had the greatest life of anyone I'll ever meet. Chad moved a community and inspired countless people to think that they can do more. He was so well respected and connected.

There were a couple hundred people at his Celebration of Life and people were coming up and saying the most remarkable things about Chad's influence on them. They were telling us stories from decades and decades prior.

When you heard Chad described by the community, they all had common themes. He had strong character and strong presence. He didn't get bullied despite being different because he stood up for himself and commanded respect. People didn't swear around him and gave him the ultimate courtesy. This went both ways. Chad respected others and he never spoke negatively of other people. He didn't judge you or criticize you — unless you were harming a plant or an animal.

After he died, I heard Chad's childhood friend explain his respect for Chad. He said that kids were mean growing up and Chad looked different than everyone else. The friend's respect grew when he saw Chad regularly stand up for himself, and most importantly, for others.

Chad mastered moderation and balance. It took him two days to eat a candy bar. Every part of his life was perfectly balanced. He enjoyed making chocolate chip cookies. It would take him two days. On the first day he made the batter and on the second he baked the cookies.

Chad didn't allow himself to get rushed. I rarely saw him stressed out or emotional. He had an ability to remain calm in a storm and by living his life with moderation and balance, he was better able to ride the waves when storms came. He didn't get lost in what had happened and didn't overthink the future to come. Chad only knew how to live in the moment.

When we find ourselves in a place of stress, it is often because we are out of balance and we swayed too far out of alignment. Chad knew how to keep life in balance.

The most profound lessons I get out of Chad's life is he worked hard at what he could do, he took responsibility for himself, he believed in himself, he never lost hope and he was determined. So many of us make excuses and say we can't do something because of this or that, and our life just isn't in the right place. I'll be the first to admit I make these excuses all the time.

We say it's not the right time, I don't feel well, I'm too busy to do this, or I'm too busy to do that. With Chad there were no days off. He worked hard every day but that doesn't mean he didn't enjoy life. He enjoyed living life and his hard work gave him purpose and value. He didn't look for tomorrow to be the day he would enjoy life. Instead, he enjoyed every moment in the best way he could.

Chad taught us that disability doesn't mean inability and also that different isn't bad — it's just different. We're all different in our own ways. We all have strengths and our quality of life isn't determined by stuff or things, by money or wealth, by fancy job titles or advanced degrees.

Instead, it is determined by the way in which we see ourselves and the world. The beauty of this is that we can all shift our perspective. We all have the ability to live our best life no matter our circumstances.

We always have plenty to be grateful for. Chad didn't see the glass as half empty or half full — he chose to be grateful for the glass being there. This made all the difference in his life.

Chadism: Chad was a true gentleman and never used profanity or judged others.

It was always a treat to spend time with Chad because when you were with him he gave you his undivided attention. He didn't get lost in other conversations or try to talk over you. He was an amazing listener.

When was the last time you had a conversation with someone and you felt heard? When was the last time you listened to a friend, not to respond, but just to listen? I know several of my friends that loved this about Chad. His patience was a gift in so many ways.
I know my parents always enjoyed mornings at the kitchen table because this is where Chad would discuss important details of his life.

CHAPTER 12

Chad's Teachings: Enjoy Life While Living It

Chad's teachings profoundly changed our family and we continue to learn from him every day. He taught our family that you don't always have to be right. I noticed a profound shift in our family when we came to the awareness many years ago: that it didn't matter if Chad saw something as the color blue if it really was black. We don't always have to be right and humbleness is a strength, not a weakness. Why would you have to rain on someone's parade? Stay humble instead. Chad helped us reach a critical point in our life where we realized compassion and understanding as fundamentally more important than being right.

One of the most significant teachings I learned from Chad is to enjoy life while you're living it. The reality is that our average day is...well, average. Learning how to enjoy life while you're living it can help you achieve balance and maximize overall happiness. On a normal day, you begin by waking up to your alarm clock and start rushing around to prepare for your day. From the moment you wake up, your day consists of a series of errands and tasks to get you from point A to point B — which often does not leave any room to stop and enjoy life's little moments.

Most of us find ourselves waiting for and looking forward to the big moments in life: graduation, wedding, the birth of your baby, that once-in-a-lifetime vacation or well-deserved promotion. I personally believe that if you are living your entire life only for those big moments, you will eventually be let down. We tend to engross ourselves entirely in the anticipation of our upcoming big event or "moment."

We focus on planning every perfect detail, building hype with our friends and family, visualizing, and dreaming of it over and over in our heads. Instead of enjoying the entire journey and the little moments along the way, we only live for that one big moment. By envisioning the perfect day so intently, we are often disappointed in the end result due to the event failing to meet the unrealistic expectations we've built up in our mind. I challenge everyone to, not only live for the big moments, but to take time to enjoy life's "little" moments too. My brother, Chad, in his infinite wisdom, showed me the benefit of living my life with this perspective.

Although he struggled with mental and physical disabilities for 38 years, as well as crippling pain as his health problems further developed, he still found beauty in the world and people around him. I found him to be a truly remarkable person, not just because he was my brother, but because he was an incredibly insightful human being. Chad was incredibly happy and peaceful in his life, despite his daily battles. He found simple pleasures in what most take for granted. He was a master at developing coping strategies to deal with his daily obstacles. Chad continually adapted and taught himself, and those around him, that life was about enjoying the journey, not just getting to the destination.

A great example of this way of living is Chad's morning routine. It would take hours, but he always made a point to enjoy the process. He would listen to music, read about Detroit sports or environmental news, and take pictures of my Mom's cat, Molly, as she laid in his sink or shower. He was content and peaceful because he found happiness in these little moments and I aspire to live more like this — to live a life with more intention and joy.

As I analyzed my own interpersonal relationships, I have discovered proof that Chad's insight was something all should live by. While helping a friend celebrate her 40th birthday, it came to me that life truly is about cherishing the little moments, even if it seems simple or mundane at first. While her guests were sitting downstairs watching the game, I stayed upstairs to talk with my dear friend while she was getting ready for her big night. What I didn't foresee at that time was that this simple moment of watching her get ready would be the most memorable part of my night as we reminisced about old times.

Don't get me wrong, I enjoyed the party very much, but months after that event, what I remembered most was our conversation while she got ready. This little moment taught me a big lesson: don't get mad at the time it takes your friends, girlfriends, or wives to get ready like most guys do. Instead, choose to be part of the process and enjoy this simple moment together rather than rushing to get to what's ahead.

With Chad's wisdom in mind, I implore you to not compare your "average" day to someone else's "once-in-a-lifetime" moment – it's just not comparing apples-to-apples. I think it's more like comparing peas to Sweet Tarts and *that* is difficult to compare properly. Sure, you can be envious of Cinderella while she attended her ball, but remember, no matter who you are, we all will have our Cinderella moments. It's easy to lose track of this as the majority of our days are spent running errands, working, cooking, doing laundry, and taking care of kids. With this, I encourage you to adopt Chad's wisdom into your routine just as I have. Start living your life with intention by cherishing and creating more of life's little moments. Those of us that master enjoying this simple lesson are one step closer to finding a true balance in our lives.

CHAPTER 13

Chad's Teachings: Life Through a Different "Lens"

After examining the effectiveness of my relationships, I found that many of the differences I have with other people are simply my misunderstanding of their perspective. I've come to realize everyone sees life through a different "lens." Our lens is shaped by many things; our background, those around us, our education, our group activities, — the list goes on and on. Because these experiences are unique to each person, it's impossible for us to see life from the same perspective.

Using mindful practices, I have discovered that instead of arguing with someone about our differences, I learn more if I simply ask, "Why?" This answer usually solves the differences between us and creates further discussion and connection. Together, we often discover that although we may do "it" or see "it" differently, the "why" is inherently the same for both of us. Sometimes, the path to getting there is much different, but we all want what's best for ourselves, our family, and our friends. Understanding the "why" is what can bring us all together.

My brother, Chad, saw the world much differently than most of us, because he was given a very unique lens. A lens that I think allowed him to give valuable and unique insight. He wanted happiness, peace, equity, sustainability, and love for every generation to come (and for his team to win the Super Bowl...of course.) No one person's path will ever be the same as ours. We should embrace our uniqueness and always keep an open mind to other's fresh perspectives.

CHAPTER 14

Chad's Teachings: Remembering Hope Perseveres

Chad was truly special. And in his life, he never lost hope. He understood that he controlled his own destiny. Every day that was a struggle, Chad had hope that tomorrow would be better than today, and the day after that would be even better yet. Hope allows us to get through life's ups and downs. None of us are immune to falling on hard times. If we zoom in on a particular moment in our life, it can look like a tragedy.

The beauty is when we pan out, our view is often much different. If we look through a wide enough lens, our life really is full of excitement, laughter, and passion. Those of us who never give up hope manage the ebbs and flows of life much easier, because (like Chad) we can see beyond the challenges of the moment and realize that life — in its totality — truly is amazing. So, no matter what life throws at you, please — *never give up hope*.

The next coffee date you have or stranger you meet, may be just the spark you need. When you least expect it, something as simple as a conversation with the right person may completely change your perspective. Let's honor Chad Hickman by remembering that although today may be tough and the thought of tomorrow may be scary, if we remain hopeful, our life has a chance of turning around at any moment.

And in that moment, we'll see things with greater clarity and it will bring the beauty and passion back in to our lives. So remember: just because something is not happening in your life right now, doesn't mean that it never will. Just have hope.

CHAPTER 15

Chad's Teaching: It's All a Matter of Perspective

What makes people, who seemingly have nothing, happy and those who seem to have everything, unhappy? It's really just a matter of perspective. How we perceive our situation determines our level of contentment. My brother, Chad, was a great example of this. He may never have been married, or formally educated, or been a strong athlete, or had a successful career — but he had so much more.

Chad was disabled and lacked mobility. He never had a formal education and never even stepped foot into a job interview or received a paycheck, but Chad's perspective was inspiring nonetheless. He learned about life by getting knocked down time and time again, but he refused to stay down. He was a great athlete in his own way and lived vicariously through Pudge Rodriquez, Steve Yzerman, and Barry Sanders. He also bowled with a 121 average. Most of us would be lucky to have a score like that.

As a career, Chad bailed cardboard five days a week at CNC National Enterprises, and during his tenure, he recycled more than 2 million pounds of cardboard. He also captured the community's admiration and respect for his environmental initiatives and inspired countless people with his determination to succeed.

Chad's situation is not unique. With the right perspective, we can all see that we have opportunities to live a happy and fulfilled life. So, next time you are feeling down about your situation, try to have gratitude for all the wonderful things you do have. This shift in perspective may make all the difference.

CHAPTER 16

A Mother's Gift

Since I was little, I remember my wise-beyond-her-years Mother telling my Dad and I: "Don't have any regrets." She meant that we shouldn't have any regrets when Chad dies. Chad was four years older than me and diagnosed with brain cancer when I was a few months old. The doctors gave him single digit chances of survival, but Chad was born determined and beat the odds.

We all knew that Chad was a miracle and my Mother wanted to protect my Dad and me. She had profound wisdom as a young mother and wife. Looking back, her continual reinforcement of not having regrets is what brings me peace. I never left anything on the table with Chad. Everything that needed to be said was said and everything that needed to be done was done. With Chad, we took the time and made every moment count. There were never excuses.

We had an amazing relationship. We weren't competitive with each other and there was genuine trust, respect, and love. We went to countless concerts, movies, and sporting events.

On a Saturday night I'd drive 45 minutes into Fremont and an hour and 15 minutes back into Grand Rapids to bring Chad to his favorite movie theatre and restaurant, even though there was a movie theatre where he lived. We went to concerts at the Van Andel arena, up north at the Little River Casino in Manistee, and all around Michigan. We often had to have handicap seating because of his unique challenges. The Joe Lewis Arena was particularly a challenge because it was built prior to the Americans-with-Disabilities Act and I had to almost carry him up to the upper bowl because the steps were narrow, it was steep, and there was no hand rail.

Reflecting, I have some of my best memories from these concerts and games that I wouldn't have otherwise attended. I could've made excuses that it was too much work or convince myself that he wouldn't enjoy these events given his challenges — but instead, I found a way to make it happen and in doing so gained so much happiness and peace.

At concerts he would stand up the entire show and sing along, pounding his fist in the air. I smile thinking about the Def Leppard concert, because although I didn't enjoy the music, I still see my brother expressing himself through song while he sang along, completely in the moment.

There is such a sense of peace that comes when you can celebrate someone's life instead of beating yourself up over things you wished you had said or done. I didn't expect my brother to die so young, but fortunately, when it came to the end of his life, nothing more needed to be said, nothing else needed to be done, and none of us had any regrets.

I miss Chad every day and talk about him as if he we're listening and I'm thankful that these experiences are joyful because we took the time to be with one another.

As I said, I didn't make excuses for not being there — I was there. When his service dog of 14 years, Gable, had reached the end of his life, I left work and joined the Family as Gable took his final breath. That night was the only night Chad ever shook my hand. As he thanked me, I could sense the respect that came from being present at such an emotional time. I may not have been perfect, but I was always present and always trying. I think being present is more important than being perfect. No matter how hard you try, an absence is still an absence and we can never recreate a moment.

It's a special feeling to not have to apologize for missing events or being late. There's a special feeling for knowing the story so well because you actively live someone's life with them. I cannot put into words the peacefulness that comes from having absolutely no regrets.

I realize that some may argue that work or life forces you to have regrets. That you would like to spend more time with loved ones but there are too many demands on your time. I challenge you to not use the words, "I'm too busy." And to stop making excuses. Life is happening right now — not tomorrow. Tomorrow may never come so if you keep putting something off you may find yourself waking up one morning and there is no tomorrow to be with someone you care about.

I hear so many stories of people who have lost a loved one and they've had regrets. Maybe it was something they wish they hadn't said or done or maybe it was that there was more to be said or done. No matter the case, these people often find themselves in their own living hell, because of the overwhelming regret that death's finality brings.

Chad taught me so many valuable lessons over his amazing life but this lesson about not having any regrets that I learned from my Mother is the most valuable of all. I incorporate this into all my relationships. I wear my emotions on my sleeve, reach out to old and new friends alike, and don't let bitterness, anger, or jealousy ruin a relationship. Losing Chad has been the most difficult thing that I have had to endure. But knowing that I had no regrets brings me a sense of peace that I will always have with me.

CHAPTER 17

Chad's Teachings: Live Life In The Moment

You don't want to get to the end of life and when looking back on it, come to the realization that you forgot to live it. Although Chad's death came way too early and no one was prepared for it, there was a sense of peace with our family because Chad had lived his life to the fullest. There was nothing more that needed to be done or said for his life to be complete, because Chad lived his life with intention and made the best of every moment. There wasn't a bucket list, a wish list, or a to-do list that needed to be done. Chad didn't say, "Well I'll be happy when I get that new job, new house or new car, or when I get married and have a baby." He didn't say I'll do that when I retire, and he didn't live only on vacation or holidays or only Friday to Sunday. Chad mastered the art of being present and because of that, he had an unprecedented quality of life given his unique situation.

In an imperfect world, Chad lived life with perfection. He wanted so little in life other than peace, unity, equity, and sustainability. He never focused inwardly on himself, instead he had compassion for everyone else, including nature and animals.

A uniqueness to Chad — and I believe a reason for his happiness — is that he lived simply. He wasn't surrounded by things and stuff or relationships that weren't healthy. He lived modestly but in doing so he found contentment and peace. This simplicity allowed him to focus on what mattered most.

When Chad drank water, he never emptied the glass in the sink if he didn't finish it. Instead he saved it for the next time. He treated the environment with the same respect we give to newborn babies — with compassion and gentleness.

It took him more than a day to eat a candy bar and whenever we went out to dinner, he always had the leftovers for lunch the next day — never wasting anything. He composted paper towels by cutting them into small squares and composted his dog Gable's hair. He even composted his fingernail clippings. Nothing was deemed disposable by Chad and he was an early adopter of environmentalism.

His ideas about politics and corporations were unique. His focus was their impact on humanity and nature. He didn't understand or get bogged down in the politics. He was more concerned in the greater impact and he took a common-sense approach. I think he felt that for most things in business and politics, people made it way too complicated.

How do I want Chad to be remembered? By throwing out traditional ideologies for success and focus in on what really matters. Never giving up, determination, respect.

What did Chad teach us about living our best life?

That giving up and quitting are not an option. To never lose hope and that working hard at what you can do is how success is measured. We all live our lives differently and need to respect the differences. Encourage everyone to have a seat at the table and give everyone a voice. Their unique insight may just change your perspective.

CHAPTER 18

Defined by Anxiety

As a child I had extreme anxiety. Separation from my parents to attend school was so provoking that I would become physically sick. I remember our neighbors would have a Labor Day fish fry every year, and the nerves would start then. Every year I still get anxiety around Labor Day and it reminds me of the near panic of going back to school I had as a kid.

I don't think my parents knew what to do with me. They bounced between caring for me and having empathy and also having the understanding that if they kept me home, it would only perpetuate the problem. As Friday got nearer, it slowly became easier to get up and go to school. But by Monday morning I started all over again from square one. I would carry a piece of my baby blanket in my pocket and carry garbage bags in my lunch pail in case I vomited on the bus.

The anxiety was so strong and so intense. It wasn't until middle school that I really started to get excited and more ready and able to go to school. Throughout my teenage years, I was a good student, missed very little school, and was very involved and engaged. Life seemed perfect the day I graduated high school.

My parents hadn't been to college and they were so excited for me to be able to attend Albion College. That fall in 1994 they moved me on campus. I still remember my Mom, Dad, and Chad moving me into my dorm. I felt their pride. My Mom made my bed one last time as her little boy. We walked throughout the quad together and they left.

The separation anxiety came back instantly.

I couldn't wait for the first weekend to come so I could go home and spend time with them. As the semester progressed, I became less confident, more anxious, and very depressed. I would sleep through class and there would be days I would hit the snooze alarm for eight hours and miss breakfast and lunch. I didn't realize how much I was struggling with depression and this extreme anxiety would become my new norm throughout adult life. I had been so excited to go off to school and become myself. The irony is that I've had debilitating mental illness from the moment I stepped foot onto the college campus.

My parents knew I was struggling. They tried their best to get me help. I went from psychiatrist to psychiatrist, from diagnosis to diagnosis, from pills to pills. I was in therapy every week and saw my psychiatrist regularly and I still struggled.

I was fortunate because I worked for my parents, so they gave me more latitude than a normal boss would. I was by and large highly functioning and when I was having good days, I found that I was very productive. After being diagnosed with many different mental illnesses, I was finally diagnosed as having Bipolar Disorder, Depression, Anxiety, and as having Obsessive Compulsive Disorder.

I remember one of my psychiatrists would write a visit summary after each appointment, and he would send it to my house. Every summary started the same with him naming all my disorders. It was so demoralizing to read these diagnoses month in and month out for years. I was forever labeled as mentally ill in my medical chart and I had begun identifying myself as anxious, depressed, and having bipolar mania.

CHAPTER 19

I'm Not Sure *They* Knew Life Wasn't Easy

For many parts of my adult life I was nearly completely disabled by mental illness. I'm not sure the world knew this though, as I had success in my work. If it hadn't been for my parent's business I'm sure I would've been fired from any other job. The beauty of working in the Family business was that they understood my potential, cared for me, and allowed me to work in a way that was fit for me.

After I stopped working for my Dad, I basically just survived. Most days I couldn't get out of bed. I had been looking for work, but I had so much anxiety and had lost so much confidence that I couldn't answer the telephone for an interview. I was broken, but I was proud and couldn't admit that I was lost. My anxiety was so extreme that I felt like I was in fight-flight-freeze mode every moment of every day. Life felt nearly impossible, and I was barely afloat. My coping skill was to freeze, so I literally shut down and couldn't get out of bed. I couldn't listen to music, watch

TV, or read. I just sat in silence with intense pressure on my chest. The pain was nearly unbearable.

Finally, I had a break after a long period of being without work and found a job with a boss other than my Dad. I was proud and excited but that was short-lived. I had not properly dealt with my anxiety and depression and the stress of a new job would eventually overtake me. I even quit once and was talked back into staying. Nobody knew that I was struggling so severely. I had learned to use migraines as an excuse early on in my life, so people were under the impression that I had chronic headaches, which I did, but that was the easiest part of my day. I was riddled with anxiety, panic attacks, and depression.

In the fall of 2013, when Chad had a stroke, I decided I needed to take care of myself, so I left this local company. Life was hard. The anxiety caused extreme pressure in my chest. The depression was so extreme I could barely get out of bed. The thought of getting ready for work seemed so daunting that I would be paralyzed to my bed. I was barely functioning, struggling to be productive, and most significantly — I lost my confidence. I lost my mojo.

Because I had had success working for my parents, I started to doubt myself. Was I right all those years to think that I was only successful because of my Dad? Was I a phony?

The day after I stopped working, I had an appointment to see a new psychiatrist. My previous doctor had retired several years earlier, and I didn't have the courage to start over. The process of finding a new doctor was overwhelming and, up to this point, I didn't have it in me to start again.

When I went for the initial appointment, a social worker asked me a bunch of questions and then recommended that I also get regular therapy. I remember in that moment looking at him and saying, "I'm not ready to be honest with myself let alone someone else, so I'll pass on therapy and I just need to get my pills." Little did I know that this was the beginning of the transformation of a lifetime.

That next year I chose to focus on myself and felt blessed that I didn't have to rush into finding a job. I spent that year with Chad and we made such great memories. The doctor had taken me off medications as I had been so over-medicated that I didn't even realize it. As the medication wore off, I started to find myself again, but it unmasked even more anxiety. Anger was my way of showing anxiety, so I was a challenge to others.

When Chad died in January of 2014, I remember the nerves, anxiety, and depression over the two months while he was dying was so extreme I would yell at nurses and I had paranoia — the world was out to get me.

I didn't have hobbies or outlets for my pain, and I was passionate about my brother, so I started writing about him. I remember the day he died I went home afterwards and wrote a post that I put on my Mom's Facebook page. Chad inspired me, and he always did. I started to find my own voice as I reflected on Chad's life from time to time. I would have moments of inspiration and write feverishly in the middle of the night on my phone while in bed. The writing was therapeutic and became a rare respite.

I was in such deep depression and denial that I didn't even realize I was struggling. In reality, I was just surviving. I'm single and an introvert with anxiety and depression, so I spent a tremendous amount of time at home, by myself, and in bed.

At the time this made me sad as I thought of all my friends out enjoying life. Little did I know that this time alone would radically transform my life and allow me to heal. In the beginning when I thought of Chad's life, I was angry at his struggles and I was mad that he had such a difficult life..

CHAPTER 20

My Radical Transformation

When I started writing more about him, a transformation took place. I began to realize that he had an amazing life. Instead of feeling sorry for him, I started to idealize him. He had complete control of his life no matter the situation.

I realized I complained about his struggles and felt sorry for him, but *he* didn't. He learned to walk *four* times and I never heard him complain. Instead he pressed on with commanding determination to succeed no matter what the new norm would become.

I had thought that his rigidity was a deficit and then saw that it actually increased his quality of life immensely. I realized that he only knew how to live in the moment and as a result, it limited the extreme downs that come from over-thinking, and as a challenge began, it gave him an increased capacity to ride the waves. He never worried about yesterday or had anxiety about the future. *He focused on what he did have and what he could do.*

My new-found understanding of Chad's life started to impact mine. I had spent so much of my life anxious about the future to the point of being physically ill. I analyzed every word I had said and would feel regret for the things of the past. Slowly my life shifted and when I heard news different than I expected, I began to react with less emotion. Now, when a struggle arrives, I don't overthink it and hold space to allow that things will work out over time. I found that often what looks like a problem at the moment, actually resolves itself.

I've taken prescription drugs for anxiety for much of my life. I couldn't live without them and would become anxious if something disrupted me from taking them. I would be looking at my watch waiting for the next time I could take my anxiety medication again. Nowadays, a long day can go by and I don't even think of taking my meds. Much of my life I was so paralyzed with anxiety that I couldn't function, and my chest would feel so tight that I couldn't breathe without lying down. I spent a huge chunk of my life in bed without the capacity to even think. I'm so grateful today because I've forgotten what that felt like.

Those who have been involved in my care heard me describe my life as always being anxious. I was defined by anxiety and never thought I'd get better. That's different today. I still have anxiety from time to time, but it doesn't overtake my life. I have control over the challenges in my life. I now have the capacity to handle any situation.

Chad was a skilled teacher and he had given me the ultimate gift. I'm not sure that he would understand all the language behind my transformation, but I know he would be proud. He cared for me so deeply. He only wanted the best for me and he would've sacrificed everything no matter the cost, to be sure of my happiness. The thing I miss most about Chad is his loyalty to me. I felt his love and support and this I carry in my heart every day.

August 22nd is Chad's birthday, and this year when his birthday came around, I didn't have any strong emotion. Initially I felt guilty but quickly thought about it, and realized that my transformation through my understanding of Chad's life had led me to be completely at peace with his loss.

I think Chad would be really happy to see me now. During some of my deepest and darkest times during the early parts of his death, I thought of how disappointed Chad would be, knowing that our family is struggling as a result of him dying.

It wasn't fair to him to put this guilt on him. He did nothing wrong, so it makes me really happy to know that I will always miss Chad, but at the same time, I will always be at peace with his loss. I don't think there's a greater gift. So many of us lose people suddenly and have regrets. Chad's death, like Chad's life, was imperfectly perfect.

The unique part of my transformation is that I've begun to see the healing in my own family. I notice my parents seeing the world differently and **reacting less harshly when things don't go as expected and** trusting more.

In some of my darker days I had so much anxiety that I remember trying online dating and being so nervous for my first phone conversation with a connection. As an aside, I wouldn't recommend online dating to someone with anxiety, paranoia, and confidence issues. That was more demoralizing than looking for work.

I wrote myself notes on what to say and what to talk about. I was so nervous to have a conversation and it's hard to even see my life that way anymore. Now I can stand up in front of a full room of people and speak for an hour and need to be almost dragged off the stage because it gives me so much enjoyment. I remember not having the courage to answer the phone when I knew had a phone interview for a job and now I'm excited to talk to anyone who will listen. I remember having so much anxiety that I was scared I'd have a panic attack on an airplane.

I remember the feelings of inadequacy and my disappointment in myself and how I felt so disconnected to the world it made me sad. I was paranoid no one liked me, and I would be depressed that I was alone. Through therapy with Dr. Post, I realized that I wasn't disconnected with the world. I was disconnected with myself. When I came to that realization, I became so content with life that I enjoy spending Saturday nights by myself.

I enjoy going to a movie or concert on my own. I'm no longer defined by what I think the world should see of me. Instead, I outwardly express my wants and needs to the world. Most of my life I was ashamed and embarrassed of my mental illness. So much so, that I specifically remember when people started telling me they saw improvements in my life that rather than feeling proud of myself, I would feel worse because then I knew I was bad or broken.

I'm now proud of my life. I understand that despite all my privilege, that yes, I did struggle and that I was deserving of love during those times. For so much of my life, I was ashamed to say I had challenges because it appeared that I had so much privilege. I thought," How could I complain? How could I be sad when so many others have it worse?"

I now ask for help and am never too proud to let someone know that I'm struggling. I realize if this book is never printed, if no one ever reads a word that I've written, I'm nevertheless grateful for the experience and my transformation.

When I say transformation, I mean transformation from a place of pity, despair, and negative self-talk to a place of gratitude, love, and acceptance. This would not have happened without writing this book.

I'm so grateful for the amount of alone time that I've had over the past four years. I've enjoyed getting lost in thought about Chad's amazing life and about my new-found perspective. Most days I don't listen to music, don't read books, or watch TV. In their place, I get lost in thought analyzing and trying to interpret my life. I'm proud of who I am and don't feel the need to apologize for who I am not.

Like Chad, I've learned to focus on what I can do and to work in the best way I can. The extreme anxiety over the past two decades used to be so severe, that I couldn't face the reality of life and the thought of getting up, showering, and brushing my teeth felt nearly impossible and I struggled with how I saw myself and how the world saw me. I was afraid to be vulnerable and I was afraid that people would see me as a disappointment. I still have those moments, but I've become resilient, and I don't get lost in those thoughts.

If you've seen me wearing a hat it's because that was the difference between me getting out of bed that morning and not. The thought of combing my hair was nearly paralyzing and would've kept me from leaving the house.

If I asked for appointments and meetings in the afternoon, it's because mornings are hard for me and I'm no longer ashamed of it. I don't have to fit into the model of early to bed early to rise.

The biggest part of my transformation has been the awareness to be who I am and learn the best ways for me to ensure success. I know my limitations, and instead of apologizing for it or feeling bad or worse, I wear them as a badge of honor and have learned work around them. The world tries to dictate who we are or who we should be, and I found the strength to be who I am — *to be proud of who I AM.*

Chad didn't worry about what the world said or how the world saw him. He focused on what he could do with what he did have.

Coming off the success of working in my Family business and struggling after I found a job with someone who wasn't my Dad, I was disappointed in myself. I thought my previous success had been a sham and was only the result of me being part of the Family business.

I struggled mentally for a long time, I lost confidence, and I no longer saw myself as being capable. Instead I saw myself as a liability and I didn't deserve anything from anybody. I saw myself as no good, bad, and broken.

Looking back on this I see these moments as a true calling and as an awakening. I no longer see them as disappointments. Now I see that I was straying from my authentic self and I was trying to be something that I wasn't.

I lost my confidence and allowed myself to be molded by those around me. I was torn between making decisions that I felt were right and making decisions that I knew others wanted me to make and I didn't have the courage or the conviction to stand up and challenge it. Now, I believe in who I am, and I know that I have the ability, and I know that I'm worthy.

The growth from these experiences is what I needed to set myself up for success. I needed to have the courage to stand up for what I believe in, and to challenge when I see something is wrong. I needed the courage to walk away when things are not right.

There's a period of my life for nearly a decade from my mid-20s to my mid-30s where I wasn't proud of who I was. I lost my own identity and was trying to be what *you* wanted me to be. I realize that the latter is an impossible way to live because the person *you* want me to be changes from individual to individual from moment to moment.

I now stand true to my convictions with courage and know who I am and who I want to be. This never changes and will provide consistency that will drive my success.

I went from living my life in such a way that every problem felt like the world was going to come to an end to a place where I am confident that things will find a way to work themselves out. I went from a place of worrying about how the world perceived me to focusing on how I perceive myself. I'm not trying to be something that I'm not. This is a peaceful way to live.

I was recently asked by a close friend if I was living my passion. The conversation came out of some of the projects that I have been working on that seemed dirty and laborious.

What I do know and am proud to say is *I'm the best toilet cleaner you'll ever hire.* I find great pride in being able to give you the cleanest toilet and I know this, because I have a client who absolutely loves when I steam clean her toilet. She tells her family that's her favorite part of TaskPro cleaning her house. I also have a client where I spent more than an hour and a half cleaning their toilet and if I had not, it would've had to be replaced.

Accepting my limitations and acknowledging who I am has given me the confidence and strength to be who I want to be. I've taken my obsessive-compulsive disorder and found a way to use that as a strength and not a weakness. Now, the days I'm the happiest are those where I can spend 12 hours getting completely lost in the detail of cleaning a very dirty home and the pride I get in the satisfaction that comes from knowing that I'm able to do the impossible and give a family their space back. It nourishes me, excites me, and is my passion.

I went from working for the weekend and dreading Monday morning by Sunday afternoon — to a place where every day feels like a weekend. I've shifted my day so I don't have to wake up to an alarm clock. I went from going to concerts and being more concerned about what happened when it ends than I would about actually enjoying the moment — to a place of contentment and just being happy for what it is. I went from always seeing the glass as half empty and worrying about not having enough — to a place where I'm just grateful for the glass being there. My transformation is not about the glass being half empty or half full, it's about being grateful for the glass.

My meditation instructor and one of the therapists on my dream team, April Kaiserlian, taught me I'm worthy of my struggles.

I felt that I had so much privilege that it was impossible for me to say that I struggled. I would have a lot of guilt and shame when I felt my life was hard. I was embarrassed to tell it to my friends and family for fear of them looking at me saying I'm not deserving of these struggles because I'm one of the lucky ones.

Awe-inspiring April showed me that I'm worthy of my suffering. She helped me accept that I am privileged and at the same time, I struggle. I can now hold both of these statements and this has radically changed my perspective.

I think so many of us get caught up in analyzing whether or not we deserve to feel bad for our suffering because so many people may have it worse. It felt so nice to understand that were all worthy of our struggles and how we perceive our situation is just as important to us as to someone else. It's not a contest to be the one suffering the most. We all deserve compassion.

Another piece of my transformation was introduced to me by the amazing Amina Knowlan. Amina speaks of the proverbial "Island of Me." Before working with Amina and the Matrix Leadership Institute, I was caught up in my struggles and felt that I was carrying my challenges alone. I couldn't see beyond my story. As I began to connect with others, I saw that we all struggle. I had been identifying myself as broken for decades. This normalized my problems and allowed me to see myself as *not* bad and broken.

It was a healthy reset and a significant boost to my confidence to understand that I'm no different than anyone else. It's ok that we struggle.

CHAPTER 21

Nathan's Teachings: You're Not A Problem To Be Fixed

Chad taught me so much about how to live my best life, but, alas, now the student had become the teacher, and I had wisdom to impart to the world.

I've been known to want to come save the day when I see others struggle. Although in my professional life as a Personal Concierge, this can be lucrative and extremely helpful to my clients and satisfying to myself, it has, at times, been harmful in my personal life. Over the past few years I have been working hard at bringing myself (or my feelings) in line with my emotions. It had not even occurred to me to do so before a special person brought it to my awareness. I'll admit it still makes me feel uneasy and I'm trying to accept it.

As an empath, I wear everyone's emotions on my sleeve and I'm particularly sensitive to the feelings of those close to me. I had a breakthrough that I want to name out loud. Someone who has had great influence on me was having a significant life challenge. After a discussion I was walking out the door, and I looked at her and said, "I'm aware you're struggling, I really care, and it's not my problem to fix."

I believe naming this to her may have been the most profound statement I've ever spoken, and it felt absolutely amazing. It brought "me" around full circle with my emotions. I had never really done that — said something like that out loud before. I was always more worried about everyone else regardless of the pain it would cause me. I felt free.

What is my takeaway? Self-love and self-compassion are not selfish. Rather, both give us the ability to hold supportive space for others by letting them know we care, that we love them, and it allows us to not lose sight of the importance of the relationship with ourselves. And the better the relationship with ourselves, the better our capacity to heal the world.

It is important for me to remember that she, along with everyone else, is not a problem to be fixed — and to remember that simply holding supportive space for her to have the experience or emotion is the most helpful thing I can do.

CHAPTER 22

Nathan's Teachings: The Key To Happiness

No one's eulogy ever describes what they had. Instead, they often describe who they were. While living the life that will become your legacy, I'd like you to consider these 3 R's: realize, remember, and refocus.

Realize: There's a credibility that comes with struggle, because only then do you truly have the ability to understand and empathize with another person. We often judge our struggles negatively — yet they have the power to direct us towards greater purpose and understanding.

Remember: All of us have at least one chapter in our lives in which we are not proud. Focus, not on the content of the dark chapters of your story, but on the growth that came in subsequent chapters.

Refocus: Our quality of life is directly related to our perception of our life. There are people who appear to have it all and are unhappy, and there are people, who seemingly have nothing, but are completely peaceful and content. It's not about competing with what others can do, instead, it's about being the best version of ourselves. Chad proved this often, because although he didn't meet society's everyday measures of success with a high-paying career, house, car, wife and kids; he was completely happy and content with everything he did have. He didn't compare himself to others. And, he was always the best version of himself. He did so by being grateful for what he did have and for what he could do.

We focus so much energy on thinking about what we don't have or on what we need to do. The mind is powerful. Remind yourself not to focus on what you don't have, but instead be grateful for everything that you do have. We all have plenty to be grateful for if we just take a moment to reflect on it. April Kaiserlian, my mindfulness teacher and "security blanket", often uses a quote from Jon Kabat Zinn in her mindfulness classes: "As long as you are breathing, there is more right with you than wrong with you."

I was practicing gratitude recently during meditation and I realized that I could have gone on for hours about what I'm grateful for. However, when I reflect on the periods of darkness in my life, that's where I lose touch with how lucky I am. The practice of gratitude has helped me to see that no matter what comes my way, I have so many blessings to be grateful for. It's allowed me to reframe my thoughts. Instead of finding bitterness and frustration in the early death of my brother Chad, I am now able to be grateful for having 41 amazing years of being inspired by and loved by my brother.

Chad, who unarguably had challenges with his health that caused him pain and gave him different abilities, was grateful for what he did have and for what he could do.

Because although he had to learn to walk four times during his lifetime, he was grateful that he could walk. Something that many of us take for granted every day. And, Chad didn't focus on why he was having problems — he focused on what he needed to do to overcome his problems.

Chad Hickman had greater character than any man I know, and his legacy will always be remembered as: INSPIRING, DETERMINED, COMPASSIONATE and always doing the right thing, even when no one was looking. And, most importantly, by being grateful for what he did have and for what he could do!

Our key to our happiness is simple…just be grateful.

CHAPTER 23

Nathan's Teachings: A World Minus Prejudice And Judgement

I have a dear little friend that often speaks of Uncle Chad. She never met Chad, but she knows how special he was. Her name is Briley, and she has changed my perspective in countless ways. She's not concerned with perceived injustices. All she wants is for me to sit next to her, play dolls and be part of her land of make-believe. She does this with everyone and in every situation. She came into this world minus prejudice and judgment and seeing the world with everyone and everything as equal.

You can learn many valuable life lessons through the innocent eyes of a child.

No filter. No bias. She's just honest with her emotions and only knows how to love. Especially in her case, she's not afraid to take risks. Briley will sing "Let it Go" from the movie Frozen to whomever will listen and will ask *anyone* and *everyone* if they want to play. She'll even share her dolls because she realizes that if she doesn't share, she'll lose an opportunity to play. Such wisdom before she is even four years old.

Briley sees beauty in everything. The snaggle toothed witch I put out for Halloween is gorgeous to her and she wakes up every day with a smile and says, "It's going be a beautiful day!" Even if it's raining and bitter cold outside.

As adults, what can we do to capture the beauty in the innocence of a child, yet do so in a chaotic world, that (at times) isn't fair? How can we not lose sight in the value of living a life without prejudice, judgment, and not fighting change? I wonder what would happen if we were open-minded to everyone and every idea? At my brother's memorial service, we played "Amazing Grace" sung by Susan Boyle. It was my choice because she, like my brother, has a remarkable and inspirational story.

On her first audition on "Britain's Got Talent," the TV captures everyone's face as they cast doubt about her ability to perform simply because of how she looked. What if she was never given a chance to sing that day? How would the lives of so many been changed? I know that I often listen to her rendition of "Amazing Grace" when I'm feeling lonely and looking for strength from the loss of my brother, and it brings me peace.

Sadly, what opportunities have we lost because we didn't give everyone an equal opportunity at the table simply because we made a decision based on prejudice or our reluctance to change? This stands true in every aspect of our lives. We are so resistant to change and so conditioned to live with prejudice that we close our eyes to potentially new and wonderful opportunities and relationships. Within seconds of seeing or hearing something different — from how we look, think and feel, we cast a cloud of doubt and judgment.

Obviously, it's difficult to maintain the innocence of a child because we are constantly experiencing new things — both good and bad. But, we can make a conscious effort to remind ourselves that everyone has something to offer and you can learn from everyone and every situation if you look at it through the right lens. My brother lived his life this way, and I strongly believe it is why he was so peaceful in his unique situation and why he had so many amazing friends.

The next time you interrupt someone's thought or idea or don't engage with someone simply because its "different," remind yourself "different" doesn't have to be bad...it's just different.

CHAPTER 24

Nathan's Teachings: Don't Just Go Through The Motions

Many average high school football players, like myself in 1994, will play in their final games during fall, so fall brings about a bit of sadness for me. As I reflect back on my life, though, I have come to realize that over my years, being an average high school football player has been my greatest accomplishment in a very good way. I particularly remember 25+ years ago, on a very hot August day, I went to my first "two-a-day" football practice. I was just entering high school and knew nothing about the game of football. With anxiety and nervousness, I took the field for the first time. I will never forget that summer day.

My dedication to football started because of a few simple, but powerful words spoken by Coach Stickney. Years later I don't remember any of our plays, not many of our drills and have no idea on how many wins or loses we had, but what I do remember is Coach yelling out in the summer heat, "Don't just go through the motions!" That phrase has stuck with me throughout all these years and not a day goes by that I don't think about Coach yelling at our team to put forth our best effort every time.

No one is immune from finding themselves sliding through life from time-to-time because we have gotten comfortable and a little lazy. I think that it would be impossible not to with the significant changes and life events that we all endure. However, when I find myself "going through the motions", I think of Coach's words and it reminds me that nothing comes easy and that you have to work hard for everything. More importantly, sometimes the reward is actually in the work itself. I think that I enjoyed football so much because it didn't come easy for me. I'm competitive, so I tried extra hard even though I may have only been considered an average player by some.

In my senior year, I was elected co-captain of the Grant Tigers, and I know that Coach had something to do with it because he knew I was exhibiting strong leadership traits through hard work. I was given this honor, not because I was the best player on the team, but because of my effort and because I lead by example. This continues to give me significant pride and a sense of accomplishment even in my adulthood.

Later in life, I started to realize that my brother lived by this same principle. Chad made every moment count. If for no reason other than his own pride and happiness. He could be proud of himself, because although he may have never cured cancer, he taught a community that you can be successful despite having cancer by having pride in yourself, always working hard, and never giving up. I can honestly say that Chad never just "went through the motions."

So, when you start your day, doing whatever it is that you do, and find yourself going "through the motions", think of Coach Stickney's words and realize you don't have to have a reason to try harder other than for yourself. No matter your skill level or talent, if you work hard today, you will always have pride in your accomplishments tomorrow and no one can take that away.

CHAPTER 25

Recognizing Gratitude

I remember growing up seeing family and friends who had "normal" brothers and sisters and I looked up to them. I specifically remember when my thinking shifted though. A friend of mine was talking to me about how lucky I was to have Chad as a brother who believed in me, listened to me, and cared about me. My friend had brothers who he had no connection to. I started to realize how lucky I was to have Chad my life. I wouldn't wish for anything different in my life.

Chad didn't know it, but he had taught me to be grateful for what I have and what I can do. I have a regular gratitude practice before I go to bed. I can lie there for half an hour and name all the ways I'm grateful. Chad and our amazing relationship are always present in the practice. When I'm in a place of crisis, this practice resets my nervous system.

I'm so blessed to have had him as a brother and as a teacher. I believe strongly that everything I have in my life and that the success we've had as a family is a result of Chad. I believe that Chad gave my parents the courage to rewrite their story and to take risks no matter the potential consequences. I believe that everything we do has a part of Chad in it and as a result our family has a greater quality of life because of him. Chad was strong and gave us strength.

I have fond memories of the music, movies, and sports we shared. We liked the same bands, enjoyed a good comedy and rooted for all the same teams. Chad was a die-hard fan of the teams he supported. Much like he lived all of his life, when he watched a game, he was completely in the moment and he was going to see it through. **Unless Chad's pain was the reason, we never left concerts early.** Chad never listened to critics or allowed them to decide what movies he would watch. In Chad's life, the game was never over until it was the last out or the clock struck zero.

What I miss most about Chad is not the movies, the music, and the excitement of the games, but the drive home. It usually took an hour. It would be silent in the car, but I knew Chad had fun during our outings. I miss walking him into the house making sure he was safely inside. He would then take off his shoes and neatly place the laces inside the shoes before he put them away. As I would leave, Chad would say, "Thanks Nathan."

I will never hear more powerful and potent words. Chad thanking me! For me, *Taking Time To-Be* part of his life was worth every sacrifice. Chad was a man of few words, he wasn't emotional, and he didn't use words he didn't mean, so I knew how important it was to Chad to tell me those words.

CHAPTER 26

Take Time To-Be, Not To-Do Became My Way Of Life

The beauty of my transformation is that, as it was happening, I didn't even realize it. The year before Chad died I decided to start TaskPro while visiting my parents in Florida.

TaskPro is a personal concierge & lifestyle management service that acts as a personal assistant to help with people's hectic lives allowing them to *Take Time To-Be*.

That year I spent valuable time bonding with Chad again. I worked weird hours from 2009 to 2012, so I hadn't spent as much time with him as usual. This was especially different because we worked together or lived together for most our lives.

During this time, I slowly and methodically laid out my vision for TaskPro. *Take Time To-Be, Not To-Do* became my slogan. My subconscious mind had planted a seed that would grow over the next few years. Looking back, I had an awareness that's Chad's success in such a harsh world was the result of living in the moment, but I didn't have a vocabulary to express it in detail. Slowly things came together.

The best part of my work is it doesn't even feel like work. My work and play are all mixed into one. In trying to help others get more time, I found my true passion.

The idea for TaskPro was born while visiting my family in Naples, Florida, in the winter of 2013. My parents had a home-watch service that monitored their home while they were gone for the season. Once a week, the service would check for leaks or concerns at their home in Naples and made sure everything was running fine. My Dad also wanted this service for their home in Michigan during the harsh winters, while they lived in Florida.

I had decided it was an interesting business opportunity and a need that hadn't been met in West Michigan, so I took a risk and founded TaskPro. The company was legally formed on May 23, 2013.

When researching more about the industry and companies in it, I found that home-watch services often go hand in hand with personal concierge & lifestyle management services. Personal concierge and lifestyle management ended up becoming TaskPro's main focus. As a trusted advisor, we also help clients with errands and tasks during the season while they are in town.

I was fortunate when Chad was dying that I could put TaskPro on hiatus and spent six weeks with my brother and then four more weeks with my parents after he died. It was such a relief to have the freedom To-Be with my family.

My parents gave me an advantage with starting TaskPro because they started Show & Tell Demonstration Service in 1978 — they gave me the tools and know-how to become an entrepreneur. I was actively involved with the family business throughout its 25 years.

The company was run out of our home for many years. I lost my first bedroom as it became the office. Nevertheless, I felt fortunate to grow up with my parents always being home. I don't know if they consciously knew they would be getting me setup for the future. They got me involved early on and I was able to hear conversations and see all the things that make a business successful. I saw all the hard work and determination behind a business. I knew the long hours they worked. My parents lived and breathed the business so at the dinner table I would hear the stories. Looking back this groomed me for today.

I grew up with an understanding of entrepreneurship and my experiences were in a wide range of areas like finance, marketing, development, bookkeeping, management, human resources, and operations. I've had certain touch points in these areas for decades.

I always knew entrepreneurship was my destiny. I remember going to elementary school and dressing up as a business man for Halloween. My Dad gave me his briefcase and I filled it up with candy and then I passed out candy to my classmates. I've always liked pleasing people.

I built TaskPro around the importance of our quality of life. We are so busy doing things that we aren't enjoying life while we live it. I figured if I can do the errands and tasks that are important in your life but don't give you value, then you can create more of your own memories.

In essence, we are a personal assistant with the ability to manage every aspect of your personal life. I find when I build relationships with families that there's an element of trust created. You become a trusted advisor much like in the corporate world you have executive assistants. The executive assistant manages your business life and knows where you're at and what you're doing. I do that on a personal level. As I learn a family's needs, I can start to predict what they need and am able to then take care of things before they even expect it.

I truly enjoy the work and doing the impossible drives me with TaskPro. When I was growing up and working for my Dad, one of the things I liked the most about my job was when I would be an assistant to my Dad. I loved being able to do the unexpected and simplify his life. This has always given me a lot of pleasure. Before I gravitated to Show & Tell when I was young, I thought a cool job would be a concierge at a high-end resort. I had even looked up what it meant to be a concierge and how to get that training when I was younger.

It is interesting how I have come full circle with it. I get to be an entrepreneur and still be that person that takes care of everybody's unique needs. It gives me a tremendous amount of pleasure. Being able to see the smile on my client's face when they're able to enjoy the moment instead of tasking on a project, lights me up. Doing the unexpected is what TaskPro is all about.

The projects we do can be as simple as waiting for a service company in the home, buying that perfect gift for a loved one, having our Chef prepare your meals, buying your groceries and putting them away, or us cleaning and organizing your home.

It goes a lot deeper than what most people at first glance think though. As I've gained trust within a family, I start to receive unique requests. We've moved families' residences where they never touched an item, bought and setup their furniture, and planned vacations.

Our attention to every detail sets us apart and is my obsession. It's a healthy way for me to utilize my OCD diagnosis. The deeper the detail, the greater the pleasure I get in the work.

The to-do-lists in our lives can become a major stress. TaskPro can take on your to-do list for you, so you can spend time with your family and friends again, or even focusing on yourself.

Creating quality time and living in the moment is the idea behind TaskPro. Chad had such a great quality of life because he didn't get lost in the complexity of the past and uncertainty of the future. Quality of life has become my obsession and I work hard to maximize my client's quality of life.

Take Time To-Be, a lifestyle movement that I created, has become my life work. Along with being an integral part of TaskPro, I will use it as a way to continue Chad's legacy and help others reclaim their life. I will continue to write about the movement on my blog TaskPro.com/blog. Additionally, I look forward to speaking events, so I can share my story through the spoken word.

I don't want us to wear our busyness like a badge of honor. I want us to move away from *doing* and start *being*. Life is happening now, and I don't want anyone to miss it. I want us to be busy…busy enjoying life. Chad's quality of life was beyond incredible despite some significant challenges because he lived only in *this moment*.

CHAPTER 27

Chad's Impact On My Clients

TaskPro and *Take Time To-Be* are influenced by Chad and we serve our clients with the guiding principles with which Chad lived his amazing life. Everything we do is about giving you more time To-Be. Chad's unique wisdom has not only guided my personal transformation, but it has also given me the tools and skillset to transform the lives of countless TaskPro clients:

> Eileen was diagnosed with cancer and I heard that she was driving herself out to the Mayo Clinic in order to have a month's worth of treatments. I reached out and asked if she would let me drive her van out there, so she could fly in, as she needed her handicap accessible van. When I got into Rochester, Minnesota, I left her van at the airport.

> When I returned to Grand Rapids that evening, I had a taxi take me to her house to pick up my car. I could tell the family was over and she was having a last opportunity to see them for a month or so. It made me feel good to know she had those

moments. Had I not taken her van, she would've been traveling that night instead of being home enjoying her family.

***

John called me from Arizona around Christmas one year. He found me online and he wanted to give his sister something special for Christmas. She works in the medical field and is extremely busy, and so he said, "I want to give her the gift of time."

We worked out a deal for a package of hours. He gave me full latitude to create a gift that he could give her. I bought a wooden box and put several unique items in it and wrote a letter about TaskPro and described what was included in the package of hours he was giving her. He came in on Christmas Eve, and I met him at his hotel. I handed the gift to him, and, when he saw the box and note, he was overwhelmed with tears of joy.

Her first use of the package of hours was to buy a gift for her brother — the same brother who bought her the gift. She called me up on a Tuesday at 3 o'clock and her brother's birthday was the next day. She had lost track of time. I was able to get a personalized gift and ship it from the UPS service center that day. Her brother had bought her a remarkable gift and her everyday life had simply gotten away. We all have times where the clock runs out.

***

Mike called from Europe where he was traveling. He was going through a stressful life change and was coming back into Grand Rapids in a few days and was moving into a new apartment. He wanted us to buy his furniture and setup the apartment for him.

When he flew in from Europe, he walked into his new apartment — fully furnished, with sheets washed, TV setup, and food and beer in the refrigerator. He could focus on himself instead of moving in.

A year later, he moved into a bigger apartment. He left on a Tuesday, and while he was away, we packed his belongings and setup his new apartment. On Thursday night he came home to his new apartment and everything was moved and organized for him. He never touched an item.

***

TaLawnda had a serious medical condition that would keep her homebound for part of the year. She wanted to reclaim her space and we went through every cupboard, every closet and organized her entire home. Although she was nearly bedridden, her house felt like a home again and she had peace of mind. It is amazing how clutter and disorganization can weigh down your mind. She didn't need more stress – her focus needed to be on getting better.

***

Alyson was moving to another state to start her life over. She was a hoarder and ready for a fresh start. She was completely overwhelmed and burned out with what needed to be done for the move. We spent 140 hours in her house. We went through the entire home with her and supported her in the process of decluttering and packing.

We knew when she needed to have a moment To-Be with certain belongings so that she had closure to move on to a new life. She was so relieved to put that chapter behind her and we gave her peace of mind. The house sold within days and she's enjoying her new life.

***

Judy had lived in her home for decades, and although the home was clean, the clutter behind closed doors had gotten away. She was planning ahead and not only wanted peace of mind for her and her husband, but she also wanted to simplify their children's lives who lived around the country — if something happened to her or her husband, the rest of the family wouldn't be overwhelmed with cleaning and organizing the house. We organized the entire home – giving her peace of mind to enjoy her home again.

***

A client was selling their home and didn't want to be involved in the process. We vetted the real estate team, helped sell the home, and moved them. Then we helped buy a new home and oversaw the renovation and move-in of the new condo. The clients were gone for the season and came home to a new home with all their belongings moved in. Knowing that they didn't have to stress out about a renovation and the process of moving gave us great pleasure, especially since the family had gone through a significant loss. They could focus on healing.

***

Jennifer had a house built and was moving into her new home. She wanted to surprise her children and move in early. It had been a stressful year for the family. We moved and assembled furniture, deep cleaned and setup the house so that she could move in earlier than expected — giving her kids a very special moment To-Be in their new home.

***

Mark's mother had passed away, and he lived out of state. It was hard enough dealing with the loss of his beloved Mother, yet her house needed work to be ready to sell. We spent 30 hours in the house meticulously detailing every room. The house sold within days and the family had one less thing to worry about.

***

Luci was moving to Chicago and needed her house deep cleaned for the new owner. The new owner was particular in their cleaning requests and the family had run out of time. We spent 30 hours on the house so that the seller had peace of mind that the new owner could enjoy their beautiful new home.

***

Elysia works long, stressful hours. Her schedule is fluid and she bounces from days to nights. She is particular about her home being clean, but it is nearly impossible for her to stay on top of the cleaning given her schedule. She doesn't need that burden. We clean her home with a special level of detail – we use high temperature steam to sterilize her hard surfaces and toilets. This gives her peace of mind and time To-Be. Her toilets getting steam cleaned are her favorite part of our service.

***

Amy and Phil bought a new house. Phil was away on business at the time of closing and Amy was overwhelmed with the condition the house was left in. As a mother and business owner, she wasn't sure how she would get it cleaned. We came in on a weekend and spent 30+ hours transforming the house into their new, clean home and she didn't have to stress out about it. She was able To-Be with her daughter and enjoy their new home, instead of laboring to clean it.

***

We get excited about the opportunity to give our clients the ultimate gift — free time and more moments To-Be.

The work we do is incredibly rewarding. We feel inspired and grateful of the trust our clients give us and we get excited to see a client's home or life transform from the work we do. We like to focus on all the details so that our clients can have the peace of mind, freedom, and flexibility to enjoy every moment.

You'll never know the value of a moment until it's part of your past, so make every moment count. TaskPro can help you enjoy more moments.

CHAPTER 28

Practicing Mindfulness Reduced My Stress

After losing my brother, I reached a critically low point and was looking for a way to bounce back. My brother had lived a very inspired and transformational life and I didn't want to let him down. His legacy was built on determination and I was determined to find peace.

This led me to mindfulness and it became a major tool that helped in my radical transformation. The practice of mindfulness is about being present in this moment without judgment.

A mindfulness meditation practice is very helpful in getting you present in the moment. There are a number of exercises that you can do. Most simply, you can use your breath as an anchor to focus on calm, relaxed breathing. You can do this while sitting, lying down, walking, driving, or standing in line. It is a powerful tool to settle your racing mind.

The body scan can also be an effective practice. You can search "mindfulness body scan" on YouTube or Google to get more information. Tara Brach has an amazing YouTube video that I would highly recommend. The video will guide you through a mindfulness practice while you explore your body — from your toes up to your head as it is in the moment — without fixing it or judging it.

Learning to "pause" throughout your day or remembering to check in with yourself before a stressful event is a great way to include mindfulness in your everyday life as well.

Continued mindfulness practice is very important, so I recommend a daily practice with an exercise that's suited to your needs. You'll be surprised how even a short practice every day can help to reshape your brain and calm your racing thoughts.

Life is meant to be lived and not to be a series of tasks, projects, to-do lists, and errands. Be sure to take time for yourself, your family, and your friends. Don't live your life in such a way that you have regrets. Be present in the moment for those who love you.

There's no doubt that all of us are busy. We are so busy that we sometimes have a second to-do list just to help us complete our actual to-do list. Our lives are consumed with lists upon lists. With so many competing demands on our time and with endless stimulus coming from 24-hour social media posts, spam email, and unlimited text messages — mindfulness allows us to settle the noise.

CHAPTER 29

Chad Would Be So Proud

I'm not sure how Chad would feel knowing he had a book written about his life and I'm not certain that he would understand the complexity of all the things I've discussed and analyzed. I do know that Chad would be proud because I finally see myself the way that he saw me. Chad was always so proud of his little brother Nathan. He took any and every moment to brag about me. He wouldn't show me love physically, but you could feel it in the room and you could feel the respect Chad had for me. He thought the world of me and it is the highest honor bestowed upon me.

Chad had such confidence in life. In his mind there was nothing that he couldn't do and that included learning to walk four times in his lifetime. It wasn't until analyzing his life while writing this book that I realized the significance of Chad's confidence in his quality of life.

For so long, I had been disappointed in who I was and didn't believe in myself, but Chad saw me through a different lens. Chad, along with my friend, Matthew

Mansfield, would encourage me through the darkness in such a way that it was hard for me to understand how they saw me as capable and worthy. I doubted their beliefs in me and I felt like a phony.

The beauty of my transformation has not just been about the resilience that I have gained but also the confidence that came along the way. I no longer look at a situation and think it's impossible. I understand, that like Chad, I have such strong determination that nothing can stop me. Chad would be really proud I finally believe in myself and that I've taken control of my life and my emotions.

Last spring, I went to see the band Styx in Grand Rapids, Michigan. This time, I went by myself. When the band played "Come Sail Away," tears came, and I was overcome with emotion. My normally shy demeanor then changed as I stood up, raised my fist as Chad would at every concert and got lost in the moment. I felt Chad's presence. The moment was indescribable, but I remember how it felt. In that moment Chad was next to me and I knew he will always be with me.

I always get goosebumps when I hear music by Styx and now I have my own version of the song "Come Sail Away":

"Set an open course for the virgin sea, CHAD'S SACRIFICES set me free, free to face the life that's ahead of me."

I'm at peace knowing that Chad's life, although challenging, was not more than he could handle. He gave me the ultimate gift — the gift to handle any struggle by shifting my perspective to the amazing life I have — and not the anxiety and depression that has weighed me down all my adult life. Chad loved me more than I could ever imagine, and his sacrifice has set into motion the ability for me to be my best self so that I can use my gift to carry on his work — his legacy — in ways he wasn't able.

CHAPTER 30

My Letter To Chad

Dear Chad,

I reflect on your life often and with eagerness and amazement. You lived an imperfect life perfectly and you showed me what integrity and character mean. You never complained about anyone other than politicians – whether democrat or republican – who didn't embrace environmentalism.

You stood up for what you believed in and never gave up hope. In your life, hope always persevered. You made every moment count and you never strayed from your convictions; ever, no matter what. You had greater character than any man I know. You had an inner understanding of what was right for mankind and treated everyone equally and with respect.

You taught the world that you didn't have to cure cancer to change the world. Instead, you showed the world how to live despite having cancer and having the odds stacked against you. Chad, I am so proud of you and even more proud that I was lucky enough to have a front row seat in your inspiring life. Even more rewarding for me; I got to be the center of it.

You persevered in countless ways and your determination coupled with your ability to handle your struggles have a way of guiding me every day. I make this commitment to you:

I will practice conservation and protect our planet.

I will respect that the ecosystem is supported by everyone and everything in it; including the water, trees, and animals.

I will remind myself that I'm cut from the same cloth as you, so determination is within me just like it was in you.

I will treat everyone and everything with respect.

I will not complain when life throws me a curve ball. Instead, I will accept that it is my responsibility to change the circumstance and press on with the commanding determination you showed the world.

I will live only in this moment and not regret or feel sorry for the past.

I will understand that I – and only I – can control my destiny, so I must always work hard.

I will have the same strong character when no one is watching as when I know the world is watching.

I will practice moderation.

I will listen deeply and intently to others.

I will give everyone a seat at the table.

I will smile no matter what.

I will never ever forget what you taught me and the community you served. It's a great reminder that one person can make a difference by working hard at what they can do.

I will never give up hope, just as you never turned off a Detroit Lions, Tigers, or Red Wings game – no matter the score.

I will never take for granted the perfect life I've been given and how you were the catalyst for all of it.

Thank you, Chad, for showing me how to live. Rest in peace my loving brother.

CHAPTER 31

Chad's Eulogy

June 22, 2014
Presented at the Dogwood Center for Performing Arts, Fremont, Michigan – By Nathan Hickman

Although I stand here today devastated by a huge loss and saddened that life has forever changed, I haven't lost sight that I am the luckiest man alive and truly honored to have been loved by and influenced by my brother. Regardless of anyone's spirituality, I believe that each of our lives has meaning and each of us have a purpose. Although Chad's path was much different than the average person, I strongly believe that he wasn't given more than he could handle. "The more difficulties one has to encounter, within and without, the more significant and the higher in inspiration his life will be." — Horace Bushnell

Chad defined excellence through his grit, courage, mental strength, and determination to make the best of each moment. As Dr. King said, "If you can't fly, then run, if you can't run, then walk, if you can't walk, then crawl but whatever you do, you have to keep moving forward." Chad never stopped moving forward.

Every moment of every day Chad was determined to succeed. To do so he had to defy the odds. When he was diagnosed and treated for cancer in 1976 at age 4, he learned to walk and live all over again — even though the doctors didn't expect him to survive. Then in 1994 when he had a serious brain injury, once again he had to learn to walk and live — never once complaining or feeling sorry for himself. In 2012 when he had a stroke, he pressed on with his commanding determination and learned to walk yet again — at home he didn't always use his walker. And a month before he died he had a rod put in his hip and even though he was dying of cancer he found the strength and pride in himself to do the impossible and learn to walk one last time. He took 19 steps.

Chad's determination and inability to accept defeat define his legacy and I hope can give others strength and courage in their own struggles. Chad's victories were the sacrifices he made to compete despite the odds. He didn't measure success by wins and losses but by will, triumph, determination, and the courage to never give up hope and never say I can't try. Chad won every morning he opened his eyes because he told the world that giving up and quitting was absolutely not an option.

Watching his success with his own struggles, Chad taught me how to live, love, and the importance of patience and understanding. The most influential thing he taught me was that you don't always have to be right and humbleness can be a strength and not a weakness. He also provided strength, love, purpose, and, most importantly, an amazing bond within our family.

Regardless of Chad's struggles, he never lost sight in the beauty that life has to offer. Chad taught me that it is not your situation or things that determine your happiness.

Instead he showed me that it is the lens through which you look that truly defines your inner peace. There are people who have it all — money, power, health, and are still unhappy and there are people like Chad who live with constant struggle, uncertainty, and pain but yet, they never lose hope and are truly happy and peaceful.

Chad's greatest gift and strongest asset were his unwavering resilience from his ability to never lose hope. Even in his final days, he never gave up. Semantics were huge to Chad. He didn't use negative words — he focused on what he could do and not on what he couldn't do. As Benjamin Hoff said in the Tao of Pooh, "You'd be surprised how many people violate this simple principle every day of their lives and try to fit square pegs into round holes, ignoring the clear reality that things are as they are." Chad understood this and instead focused and worked hard on what he could do.

Chad taught the world how to live despite having the odds against him. Every day was a struggle but those around him never knew it because he didn't complain, was grateful for what he did have and for what he could do. He made the impossible possible simply by being hopeful that by working hard and never giving up the next day would be better than today. And the day after tomorrow will be better yet. Chad always had goals and he never lost sight of what was needed to accomplish each of them. In Chad's life, hope always persevered. Chad was truly a gift to anyone who crossed his path.

Chad's life was far from perfect, but he lived it with perfection. Under conditions that most would say, "I quit," Chad quietly rose and told the world: "I will not be defeated." He understood that although he could lose his physical strength to illness that nothing could beat his superhero-like mental toughness.

Chad was always in the present. Never worrying about yesterday or tomorrow, but just enjoying the now. He didn't talk on his cell phone during a movie or dinner. When you were with Chad you always had his undivided attention.

Chad found pleasure in what we take for granted. His morning routine took hours, but he enjoyed the process. Listening to music, reading, and taking pictures of Mom's cat Molly in his sink or shower and sending them to Mom and me. When we went places sometimes we would forget to tell Chad where we were going. He'd get in the car anyway. Despite not always knowing the destination, Chad enjoyed the journey and the memories we made along the way.

Despite the pain and challenges, Chad found joy in life and I am happy that I was a big part of that. Many of my fondest memories are with Chad. We shared sports, music, and movies. Chad enjoyed comedies, classic rock, and was a dedicated fan for all Detroit and University of Michigan sports. He always knew the score to every game and on NFL draft day, he was glued to the TV because he had faith that *this* draft class would finally bring a championship to Detroit.

We had the opportunity to see many great concerts: Kiss, Motley Crüe, Aerosmith, Journey, REO Speedwagon. Chad learned to write athletes he liked and admired while in John Mooy's class back some 30 years ago. His collection of autographs is impressive. In this era, people would never send out handwritten letters. Chad hand wrote, in pencil, to people he liked an admired for over 30 years. He met Wayne Fontes, Herman Moore, and Barry Sanders. President Obama wrote him a letter in response to Chad's thoughts on his environmental policy. Once while in the hospital Chad got to meet Lomas Brown, a Detroit Lion's player. Even he was inspired by Chad's story.

I never heard Chad speak negatively about anyone other than the Cowboys, the Spartans, and politicians, whether democrat or republican, who didn't embrace environmentalism. Chad was destined for greatness. Chad Hickman was an environmentalist. Chad knew right from wrong and would never waiver — to him the world was black and white. There was no grey. It was either right or wrong and if it destroyed the earth or harmed a plant or an animal, no matter the cost, it was wrong. He understood the importance of nature and protecting our environment. He was talking about the importance of environmentalism before it even became a buzz word — before politicians and the media started talking global warming, Chad was talking conservation. He composted, recycled, grew his own garden, and conserved water.

He had greater character than any man I know. He wasn't influenced by popular opinion. Instead he relied on his inner understanding of what was right for mankind and never gave in. He had a heart so big that he would be frustrated when a limb was cut from a tree. In his eyes, the tree was there before us, did nothing wrong, and most importantly, provided us with the oxygen and shade that we need to live. To him, we are all one.

Thank you, Chad for teaching us the value of innocence and civility. You also showed us that it truly is the simple things that make us happy. You will be missed but I promise you and your legacy will never be forgotten.

I want to thank my parents for showing all of us, by their example, the definition of love, dedication, and sacrifice. Chad was strong, but my parents gave him strength. Chad was happy because my parents gave him opportunity and never saw his challenges as a reason to not let him live the best life he could. My parents gave Chad the best possible quality of life given his situation. Even though he had seizures, they allowed him to swim in the river and even though he had no sense of direction, they allowed him to guide me throughout 40 acres of wooded property as we were growing up. By today's standard they may look crazy, but to me, they are the perfect parents because Chad grew up focusing on what he could do rather than on limiting his life with concern over what may possibly happen. They were always concerned but they never let that keep Chad from living a happy and normal life.

Chad gave me hope and it is through his teachings that I'm hopeful that our family will be fine. Chad taught me patience and understanding and an appreciation for being different. Most importantly through Chad I learned that disability doesn't mean inability. We all do things in our own different way — not right or wrong, just different. Chad showed me that we all need to have patience and understanding in others, allow everyone to speak and have their turn, and remain open minded — different isn't bad — it's just different. Chad, I am who I am because of you — you have given me strength and courage and most near to my heart — the confidence in knowing that you loved me and want nothing but the best for me. Chad, I make this promise to you: No matter what life throws at me, I will carry on your legacy and press on and remember quitting is absolutely not an option. I also will never lose sight of the pleasure of being in the moment and in the journey.

CHAPTER 32

The Chad Hickman Legacy Fund

Chad's impact on the world was profound and as a Family we wanted his legacy to live on not just beyond his death, but also beyond ours. The Chad Hickman Legacy Fund is an endowment at the Fremont Area Community Foundation. The fund's purpose is to carry on Chad's lifelong work as an environmentalist, to keep his strong spirit alive, and continue his teachings.

The first contribution from the Chad Hickman Legacy Fund was to help the City of Fremont rebuild a bridge in Branstrom Park. Chad loved the park, as he loved all nature. The contribution was as much a thank you to the community for giving Chad an incredible quality of life as it was a way to honor his legacy.

The sign on the bridge near the front of the park's entrance reads:

Chad Hickman's Bridge of Hope: No matter our circumstance, Chad taught the community that HOPE always allows us to persevere.

In Chad's life hope always persevered — the story
of hope defines Chad's legacy.

Epilogue

My highest honor was the opportunity to eulogize my brother's amazing life. In 41 years, he accomplished more than most under circumstances that seemed impossible. I proudly speak of often, and I learn from him every day. My favorite part of any day is getting lost in my reflections of his profound life.

Chad had more setbacks than most people could imagine yet he also had the highest quality of life of anyone I know. Why? Because:

He took complete responsibility for his life and happiness. He was determined no matter the circumstance.

He lived a life of balance and moderation. It would take him days to eat a candy bar. He'd eat it a section at a time.

He was grateful for what he did have and for what he could do

He never spoke negatively of others

He lived only in the moment. Hence *Take Time To-Be* was born.

What do I want you to remember from this book?

I'm devastated that I lost my brother and I am at peace with his death. Why? Because I was blessed with my Mom's teaching to never having any regrets. When Chad reached the end of his life, everything that needed to be said was known, the memories had been permanently recorded, and I knew nothing was left on the table. This is an amazingly freeing feeling. By being in the moment in your life, maybe you can find peace too.

Borrowing a quote from Chad's lifelong friend and teacher, John Mooy, "This isn't a story about how he left us. It's a story about how Chad Hickman lived and OH HOW HE LIVED!"

ABOUT THE AUTHOR

Nathan Hickman
Founder + Personal Concierge & Lifestyle Manager,
Author, and Speaker
TaskPro, LLC

Phone: 844-4-TASKPRO

Email: hello@taskpro.com

Web

taskpro.com

Videos

taskpro.com/videos

Blog

taskpro.com/blog

LinkedIn

linkedin.com/in/nathanhickman

Facebook

facebook.com/thetaskpro/

facebook.com/taketimetobe/

Book

taketimetobe.com

Brochure

taskpro.com/brochure

Made in the USA
Middletown, DE
12 April 2019